MONDAY
MORNING

Customer Service

David Reed and David Cottrell

CornerStone
Leadership Institute

www.**cornerstoneleadership**.com

MONDAY
MORNING
Customer Service

Inquiries regarding permission for use of the material contained in this book should be addressed to:
CornerStone Leadership Institute
P.O. Box 764087
Dallas, TX 75376
888.789.LEAD

Printed in the United States of America
ISBN: 0-9746403-2-8

Credits
Editors   Alice Adams
                                                 Sue Coffman
                                                 Cal & Millie Reed
Design, art direction, and production   Back Porch Creative

———◆▸〉◀◆———

"The highest
of distinctions
is **service**
to others."

– King George VI

———◆▸〉◀◆———

Introduction

Six months ago, the changes started...in my career...in my priorities...and my life.

As senior manager for the Harris Hospitality Co., I was responsible for financial planning for several diverse businesses, including Fiesta del Sol, a small theme park. When my kids were younger, our family frequented Fiesta del Sol on weekends, and we all had great memories of our visits.

The weekend some of our closest friends, Tim and Leslie Hatfield, were visiting from Chicago, we thought it would be fun to visit the park, so early Saturday morning we loaded our SUV and headed for a day at Fiesta del Sol.

I was proud to show off the park and enjoy the day with our friends. Fiesta del Sol had always been a fun place for people of all ages, particularly because the employees were friendly, service was excellent, and it seemed that everyone at the park was focused on making each guest's experience enjoyable.

Shortly after we walked through the gates, however, I began to realize that things had changed.

The once-friendly employees now seemed to be bothered by the guests. The service that I remembered as excellent was now nonexistent. Instead of pampering guests and making sure each visitor enjoyed the experience, park attendants seemed to resent having to be there.

I was stunned!

Attempting to make excuses and justify the lousy service we were receiving, my words fell flat. Worse than that, I could see that Tim and Leslie were not having any fun at all. Needless to say, I was embarrassed to be associated with Fiesta del Sol and apologized to our guests as we hurriedly left the park.

The experience at Fiesta del Sol bothered me, really bothered me. How could a place that I had enjoyed so much in the past become such a disappointment? How could once stellar service drop to what I considered "nonexistent"?

I had seen the park's numbers decreasing for months on the financial reports that crossed my desk, but I had bought the "economy is bad" excuse. Now I realized that more was involved than the sluggish economy.

For the remainder of the weekend, I wrestled with what I should do — or say — about my disappointing experience at Fiesta del Sol. After all, I am a manager and have an obligation to share both good and bad news during our weekly staff meetings.

After more thought, I decided to prepare a detailed report about my experience and present it to the team.

That week, I sat in my regular seat where I had given my financial reports each Friday for almost two years. On many occasions, I had been the bearer of bad news as I announced the need for budget cuts or personnel reductions. This meeting was going to be different.

I was still upset — no, I was still incredulous — about the disappointing experience at Fiesta del Sol with my friends, and I was determined to make sure our operations team knew the good, the bad and the ugly of our visit there.

When it came time for my report, I used a tone different from that which people around the table were accustomed to hearing. "Before giving my financial report, I need to discuss something very personal, very important," I began, and then proceeded with the details of my experience and how embarrassed I had been with the level of customer service.

"When I took my family to the park years ago, things were different," I continued. "We were always treated as special guests, and that made me proud to be part of this organization."

The room grew still, and it soon became apparent I was verbalizing what many other members of the leadership team had been feeling. When I finished my comments, all eyes were on Madeline Baker, Harris Hospitality's CEO.

Madeline was a quiet, thoughtful leader who had gained the respect of the team by using innovative approaches to continuously improve each of our businesses.

She sat quietly after I finished my presentation — as did the rest of the group — for what seemed to be an eternity. (I have to admit, at that point, I was questioning whether I should have been so bold in my statements.) Then the CEO smiled and said she appreciated my honesty.

"As all of you know, Jerry Mills served our company well for 25 years as director of Guest Services for Fiesta del Sol," Madeline began. "He retired last year, and we haven't named a replacement. As you also know, I'm a firm believer in shifting leadership responsibilities around now and then. It keeps us from getting stale."

It was at this point that my career changed.

Madeline looked in my direction. "Brett, thanks for bringing this situation to our attention. I can tell you have a passion for this part of our business, and while I normally don't have this type of discussion in a group, I feel strongly about this idea. Would you be willing to assume the role of director of Guest Services and help return the level of service at the park to one which you will again be proud of?"

I was shocked!

I had spent my entire career sitting on the sidelines and crunching numbers. Was I capable of taking on a gigantic new job on the front lines?

Then, from somewhere deep within my soul, I felt my enthusiasm rising to the challenge. Was it time for such a radical career change?

I looked around the table. My colleagues were smiling encouragingly. Was this a sign of their support, or were they trying to dodge this loaded gun? At any rate, I decided to take on the challenge.

Later that afternoon, after Madeline and I met to work out the details, a memo went out to all employees, announcing my appointment as director of Guest Services. It was a done deal.

When I arrived home that evening and told my family what had transpired, it all began to hit me. It was one thing to be a guest at Fiesta del Sol Park and offer advice, but what did I know about improving customer service?

Panic set in. What had I done?

Before the staff meeting that day, I had a stable position in my area of expertise. In six weeks, I would move into a new office and take over a new set of responsibilities.

Late that night, after all the lights were off, I talked about my fears and concerns with Lisa, my wife, who made a suggestion that would give me a shot at success in my new role. "Remember Sam Baldwin?"

"Wasn't he general manager of the downtown hotel we visited for years on our anniversary? You may want to call him and get his advice. You always remarked after our weekends there that they had the best customer service of any place we'd stayed."

"Great idea. In fact, I think he retired last year. He would be the perfect person to help me. I'll give him a call tomorrow," I said sleepily.

The next morning, when I called Sam, I explained the circumstances leading up to my new job. He laughed and immediately said the words I was waiting to hear: "I'd be honored to do what I can to help. Once we traveled awhile and I relandscaped our gardens, retirement has offered little in the way of challenge, so I welcome this project.

"Why don't we meet at my beach home until you feel comfortable with your new job?" Sam suggested. "Of course, it will take a significant time commitment for both of us, so I suggest we block out two hours at the same time every week. How does Monday morning work for you?"

"That would be great! Can we start tomorrow?" I asked, making no effort to hide my excitement.

"Boy, you are anxious!" Sam laughed. "I have something scheduled for the next two Mondays, but we can start after that. How about 8:00 a.m., beginning Monday the 21st?"

That was it...the beginning of an auspicious journey, well worth the time and effort it took in reaching the destination.

The following pages contain the wisdom and guidance Sam shared with me during our Monday morning meetings, and after a little practice, I've found that the truths Sam shared are applicable to any business in any sector of the marketplace.

It is my hope that this account of my meetings with Sam will make as significant a difference in your career as it has in mine.

The First Monday

Listen Up!

I don't recall ever being so anxious for a Monday morning to arrive! I had spent the past two weeks thinking about my new position, anticipating the possibilities. Part of me was excited and ready for the challenge. Another part felt very ill equipped and unprepared for such an important role.

On the 21st, I woke before the alarm rang and left early for my first meeting with Sam. Knowing that Sam was always there ahead of time at every event where I had seen him, I didn't want to take the chance of being late.

Traffic was lighter than normal, and I arrived in Sam's neighborhood with 30 minutes to spare. I pulled my car into a parking lot around the corner and thought through some of the questions I wanted to ask Sam. Then I sat quietly. I had not felt this mixture of emotions since the night before my first day of college.

The scheduled time arrived. I pulled around the corner and walked toward Sam's door. He saw me approaching and met me halfway down the walkway.

Sam was tall, handsome and sturdy for his age, with an athletic build and a stylish goatee. It was obvious that he still exercised regularly.

"Great to see you, Brett! It's been too long."

I gave Sam a firm handshake. "Thank you so much for agreeing to meet with me," I said. "Just knowing that I'll be able to learn from an expert gives me hope that I have a shot at being successful in this career shift."

"Well, I don't know if I'm an 'expert,' but I am willing to share what I know. Come on in. I thought we'd sit out on the back deck. Would you like some coffee?"

Sam had a fresh pot waiting for us on the deck that overlooked the Atlantic Ocean. The only thing separating us from the ocean was a small sand dune.

"This is a great place, Sam!" I said. "How long have you owned it?"

"It's been in my family for three generations. It may not be the most modern of homes on this stretch, but it has a lot of memories. Here, let me show you around."

I followed Sam into the house and into an impressive library.

"I'm particularly proud of the collection of management books I've amassed over the years," Sam said, "but my pride is my collection of autographed editions, some going back to the 1700s."

I took one of the books on the shelf, a copy of a Tennessee Williams' play, *A Streetcar Named Desire*, one of the newer editions of the collection. Turning to the flyleaf, I saw Williams had scrawled his name and dated it.

Then my eyes wandered to several shelves of plaques and trophies. "What are these, Sam?" I asked.

Modestly, he described some of the various awards he had received over the years, not the least of which was "Man of the Year" from the national Chamber of Commerce organization.

There was also a collection of photographs, some of Sam's family, but others of Sam and Washington bigwigs, corporate chairmen and a few Hollywood celebrities. One photo of Sam and a man I recognized as a leader in the automobile industry was inscribed, "To Sam Baldwin, a winner in every sense of the word when it comes to teaching customer service."

"Mmm. Very impressive," I finally managed. "This looks like a comfortable place to spend time."

"My favorite. That's why I showed it to you first," Sam said. "Now let's do a quick tour of the rest of the place. You'll have to see Becky's folk art collection. She's really worked hard and is very proud of it."

A few minutes later, we were back on the deck, and my host was warming up our now-cool coffee. Ready to get started?" Sam was refreshingly enthusiastic.

I launched into my first question. "I know the importance of providing excellent customer service from my own experiences as a consumer, but if I'm going to be director of Guest Services, I should be able to tell my team why it's critical to excel in this area. You've been so successful in your career that you must have some tips to share."

Sam took a sip of coffee and then leaned back in his chair. "For years, companies of all types focused their attention and resources on gaining market share by bringing in new customers. Then several years ago people starting realizing that spending some of their funds and energy on retaining their existing customers would pay big dividends.

"Think of a large bucket with the marketing efforts focused on 'pouring' new customers into the top of the bucket. The problem was that there was a huge hole in the bottom of the bucket, and customers were leaving as quickly as they were coming in the top."

Sam continued. "Experience proved that it takes up to six times more effort to get a new customer than it does to maintain existing customers. Your existing customers are a valuable source of referrals, and they're comfortable doing business with you. They generally require less of your attention in order to keep their business."

"That makes sense. So what you're saying is that for my position, I need to develop a process that keeps my existing customers happy enough to keep coming back."

"I like the old saying, 'There's always room for improvement. It's the biggest room in the house,'" Sam chuckled, and then resumed his point. "We'll talk about some specific ideas in this arena in a few minutes." Sam took another long sip of his coffee. "But right now I have a question. How long do you think it took to get a new product developed and to market, let's say, 10 or 15 years ago?"

I was puzzled. Where was Sam going with this? "I don't know," I fumbled. "I would guess several years, depending on the industry."

"You're close. Now, what do you think that time period would be for a similar product today?" Sam asked again.

"Probably a few months to half a year."

"Your answer is in the neighborhood. So, what do you think that means as far as the importance of customer service?" Sam questioned.

"I'm not sure I see the connection," I replied, a bit confused.

"Let me explain. In the past, a company could create a unique product or offer a new service, and it would take their competitors years to match it and provide true competition. The company with the innovative edge would gain a large number of customers in the interim, regardless of their customer service."

A light came on. "Okay, I think I see where you're going with this," I responded. "In today's market, a company can create a new product, and another company could match that offering in a very short time period."

Sam continued his questioning. "What do you think would differentiate one company from another if they have almost identical products?"

"The obvious answer is customer service," I said, confident that I was catching on. "The company that has the best employees and can meet the needs of the customer, especially when there's a problem, is going to gain the largest market share."

"You got it," Sam said. "Okay, now here's a no-brainer. A big reason that excellent customer service is so important is that angry customers talk!"

"I know that's true," I chimed in. "I had such a bad experience at a seafood restaurant — food poisoning — a few weeks ago that I made it my mission to let people know about it."

Sam continued. "The average unhappy customer will tell as many people as they can about their experience, and the hard part about this is that very few unhappy customers will tell the company or restaurant or hotel they're unhappy. They'll just stop doing business with that establishment. It's a fact — good customers are often the ones that can kill your business. These customers are so nice and so good that they won't tell you — before they leave — what's gone wrong or why they're leaving," he added.

"Wow. So how do you find out how your customers are feeling about your product or service?"

"Every organization that wants to be at the top in their field understands the importance of gathering feedback. This can be something as simple as placing a customer feedback card in key locations in your facility or with each product you sell," Sam explained. "The only problem with leaving it up to your customers to complete a card is that, as I mentioned earlier, most customers will not take the time, and the difficulty with being in a leadership position is that the higher up you go, the less likely you are to hear the truth.

"In most cases, there are many filters between the customers' communications and what the CEO gets to hear. In fact, most middle managers make sure the CEO only hears positive feedback, the good stuff customers have to say. The more negative it is, the more certain you are that it may not even reach your middle-management levels. Even so, in a leadership position, it's important that you position yourself to glean as much direct customer feedback as possible because you can gain some important information using this method," he said.

"If you don't get great results from the feedback cards, what else do you recommend to find out how your customers are really feeling?" I questioned.

Sam took another sip of his coffee and started explaining another process that he had used often.

"Over the past 40 years, I've gathered customer feedback in a variety of ways, but the best results were achieved by having an independent group come in, meet with my employees, customers and partners, and conduct surveys. This could be an outside consultant or one of your peers from another part of the company. The key is finding someone who is not part of your day-to-day operations so they will ask important questions and provide honest feedback, even if it's not very positive. Do you have a friend in another department you could work with on this?"

I thought for a minute. "Yes, there's a guy in a similar role in one of our hotel properties, Randy Inman. He's in Atlanta, but

I could talk him into coming down and performing an independent assessment."

"Sounds like the perfect person," Sam said, adding another dollop of his enthusiasm. "Why don't you give him a call and schedule a visit? Good input will help you come up to speed quickly if you get it fairly soon after you start a new position. Also, as you begin, you'll also be more open to ideas before you start forming your own opinions about operations," Sam said.

I was intrigued by this approach, but puzzled by one thing. "I thought you were interested in identifying how your customers felt," I quizzed. "Why did you interview your employees as part of this process?"

"That's an excellent question — and here's the answer. Over time, I have found that most of the great ideas for improving customer service come from the employees who spend the most time with the customers. It's hard for those in leadership positions to stay in touch with the customers, and it's even harder for senior leadership to stay in touch with customers. Then, too, I have found that most employees were actually excited about finally having their opinions considered!"

"So did you find that your employees and customers were more likely to give honest feedback to someone outside of your department?"

"Here's what we did. We introduced the individual to them and assured them that we were genuinely interested in their honest and blunt feedback. That individual then conducted surveys and met with key customers to conduct interviews and listen to their comments.

"We also benefited in another way." Sam's eyes sparkled. "Most of our customers were impressed that we were going to such effort to find out how to serve them better. This process alone improved our relationships with many of our best customers."

"Okay. I understand the need to gather this data, but what do you do with it once you have it?" I asked.

Sam smiled. "Another great question — and this is where many companies fail. Once you've gathered the data, it's critical that you use this information to make changes in your products and services. You're better off not asking your customers for feedback if you don't plan on using it to make changes.

"Another important point about this process is that I had an individual responsible for working with operations make changes based on the trends and data we gathered. When you do this — make changes — it's critical to have the full support of senior management and to make sure the employees involved understand why change is needed."

"You want to know another trick?" Sam asked.

"Sure," I said as I moved forward in my chair.

"I call it 'closing the loop.' It's important to let your employee, customer or partner who offered the feedback know that you heard them, and, when possible, tell them what changes you're making to address their concerns. I've found that a few well-placed return phone calls will pay big dividends, and you'll have some amazed customers. They never expect that you'll really listen and actually respond."

"That's great, but you can't run around responding to every client comment. How do you decide what to act on and what to ignore?"

"Another great question. You're getting the hang of this quickly," Sam said. "The leadership team reviewed the survey data and feedback cards, identifying the major issues and trends. We don't always make changes based on every complaint, but when we find several customers saying the same thing, we stand up and take notice."

Sam led into his next point. "Another important aspect of listening to your customers falls on the shoulders of the leadership team. Many leaders get so caught up in the paperwork and personnel responsibilities of their job that they forget to spend time with their customers."

"So, how much time do you recommend, and how should I make this happen?" I asked.

"I've always scheduled half a day twice a month for spending time with my customers. I'm not talking about having executive conversations, but actually spending time with the people who use our product or those that are our paying guests," Sam replied. "This gives you firsthand knowledge of the issues and challenges facing your organization. Customers appreciate an executive taking this kind of time to truly seek their opinions about how to improve the product or service. And best of all, it's fun!"

"Were I a gambling man, I'd also bet those frontline employees appreciate their leader spending his or her time walking in

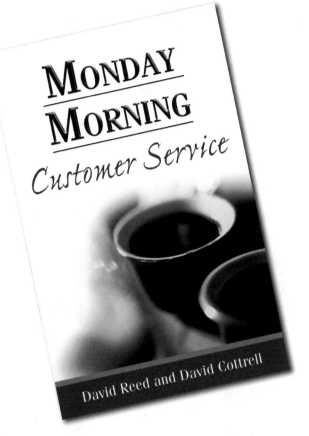

MONDAY MORNING *Customer Service*

David Reed and David Cottrell

3 Easy Ways to Order
Copies for Your
Management Team!

1. Complete the order form on back and fax to 972-274-2884

2. Visit www.cornerstoneleadership.com

3. Call 1-888-789-LEAD (5323)

CornerStone
Leadership Institute

Amazon Top 5 Leadership Book!

Monday Morning Leadership is David Cottrell's best-selling book. It offers unique encouragement and direction that will help you become a better manager, employee, and person. **$12.95**

Goal Setting for Results addresses the fundamentals of setting and achieving your goal of moving yourself and your organization from where you are, to where you want (and need) to be! **$9.95**

136 Effective Presentation Tips provides you with inside tips from two of the best presenters in the world. **$9.95**

Sticking To It: The Art of Adherence reveals the secret to success for high achieving organizations and provides practical advice on how you can win the game of business. **$9.95**

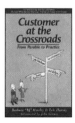

Listen Up, Sales & Customer Service is written from the perspective of a customer who cares enough to tell you the truth. This book maps a step-by-step pathway to long-lasting customer relationships. **$9.95**

Building Customer Loyalty provides 21 essential elements that build Customer Loyalty. You will also learn dozens of ways to strengthen your customer relationships. **$9.95**

Customer at the Crossroads offers a humorous and entertaining way to reinforce key customer service values. **$9.95**

180 Ways to Walk the Customer Service Talk is one resource that you will want to read and distribute to every person in your organization. It is packed with powerful strategies and tips to cultivate world-class customer service.
$9.95

175 Ways to Get More Done in Less Time has 175 really, really good suggestions that will help you get things done faster… and usually better.
$9.95

Monday Morning Customer Service Package

$99⁹⁵

☑ **YES! Please send me extra copies of *Monday Morning Customer Servic***
1-30 copies $14.95   31-100 copies $13.95   100+ copies $12.95

Monday Morning Customer Service	_____ copies X _____	= $_____

Additional Recommended Reading

Monday Morning Leadership	_____ copies X $12.95	= $_____
Goal Setting for Results	_____ copies X $9.95	= $_____
136 Effective Presentation Tips	_____ copies X $9.95	= $_____
Sticking To It: The Art of Adherence	_____ copies X $9.95	= $_____
Listen Up Sales & Customer Service	_____ copies X $9.95	= $_____
Building Customer Loyalty	_____ copies X $9.95	= $_____
Customer at the Crossroads	_____ copies X $9.95	= $_____
180 Ways to Walk the Customer Service Talk	_____ copies X $9.95	= $_____
175 Ways to Get More Done in Less Time	_____ copies X $9.95	= $_____
Monday Morning Customer Service Package	_____ packs X $99.95	= $_____
(one of each of the 10 items above)	Shipping & Handling	$_____
	Subtotal	$_____
	Sales Tax (8.25%-TX Only)	$_____
	Total (U.S. Dollars Only)	$_____

Shipping and Handling Charges

Total $ Amount	Up to $50	$51-$99	$100-$249	$250-$1199	$1200-$3000	$300
Charge	$5	$8	$16	$30	$80	$12

Name _____ Job Title _____

Organization _____ Phone _____

Shipping Address _____ Fax _____

Billing Address _____ Email _____

City _____ State _____ Zip _____

❑ Please invoice (Orders over $200) Purchase Order Number (if applicable) _____

Charge Your Order: ❑ MasterCard   ❑ Visa   ❑ American Express

Credit Card Number _____ Exp. Date _____

Signature _____

❑ Check Enclosed (Payable to CornerStone Leadership)

Fax	**Mail**	**Phone**
972.274.2884	P.O. Box 764087	888.789.5323
	Dallas, TX 75376	

their shoes," I offered.

"That's another important benefit," my mentor agreed. "If a leader doesn't regularly spend time with the frontline employees, they often make the complaint that their leader 'has no idea what happens in the real world.' Have you ever heard that statement?"

"I sure have. I remember using it myself, earlier in my career," I confessed. "We had an executive who would stay in his office and issue new policies that made our work more difficult. The entire team felt that he was not qualified to make these decisions because he had no contact with our guests. In fact, most of those employees quit and went to work somewhere else. Why? Because people quit people. They don't quit policies or strategies. They quit people."

Sam looked at his watch. "Well, Brett, I think we've covered a lot of ground for our first session. Why don't you summarize what we've discussed?"

I was just getting started and realized how much I had to learn. "You're right, Sam. I'm probably close to capacity, but I'm taking several points from this first meeting:

1. Customer service is critical to a successful operation. Most unhappy customers will not mention they are not pleased. They'll simply take their business elsewhere.

2. It is a good investment to spend resources to retain existing customers. Your best customer is your current customer.

3. It is important to have a complete closed-loop process to gather feedback, take action and then respond to the customer.

4. You should use a combination of internal feedback tools and external resources to obtain a good balance of data. An independent assessment is a good process for obtaining an accurate picture of how you are doing.

5. All leaders should schedule regular time with frontline workers and customers to stay in touch with current issues and challenges.

6. "People quit people."

Sam stood and extended his hand. "Excellent job, Brett. Sounds like you've got it. Now, before next week, I'd like you to take a look at your department's current process for gathering customer feedback. Then, next week, let's talk about the value of 'shopping your competition.' Also, why don't you try to get out of the office and spend a few hours with your main competition?"

"Sounds like a great next step, Sam! I'll see you next week... and thanks!"

I left Sam and headed for my car, excited about our discussion, but wondering if I would have time to learn the basics before starting my new position in four weeks.

The Second Monday

Scout the Competition

That week went by quickly, and soon I was making the drive to Sam's beach house again. The air was thick with humidity, and roiling gray clouds framed the surf.

"Hello, Brett. How was your week?" Sam opened the door as I walked up the sidewalk.

"Great! And what have you been up to?" I asked.

"Well, you know, retirement is tough," he began. "I had to play golf twice this week, once in a charity tournament sponsored by my former employer."

"Man, what a life," I thought to myself. "It'll be a few years before I can enjoy that lifestyle, and unless I figure out this new job, the only golf I'll be playing is Putt-Putt."

It was a rare rainy day, so we decided to meet in Sam's office instead of on the deck.

"Can I pour you some coffee?" Sam asked.

"Sure!" I said, sinking into an overstuffed chair next to his desk.

"Well, did you get a chance to scout your competition this week?" Sam set the steaming mug next to me and took his place in his chair.

"I sure did...and I learned more than I thought I would."

"Tell me about it." My mentor had a way of getting right to the meat of our planned discussion.

I spent last Saturday with Lisa and our kids — Tony and Holly — at Fantasy Vista, a resort just a few miles from my company's facility. I hadn't been there since I started working for Harris Hospitality. I think part of me felt that I shouldn't contribute to the financial success of my main competitor.

"Anyway, we pulled up at the entrance, and the valet parking attendant opened our door. I was curious, so I asked the attendant some basic questions about the amenities of the resort. He was polite, but basically said, 'I'm not sure, sir. I just handle the cars.'"

"How is that different at Fiesta del Sol?" Sam asked.

"Well, I realized that even though I was not pleased with the overall service when I took my friends to the park, the valet service at Fiesta del Sol does a great job. They are employees of our company, not a contract valet firm. We send them through the same orientation that all of our service employees attend," I said.

I knew a number of resorts had begun using contract firms, so I asked Sam what he thought about outsourcing.

"That's a tough area, Brett, and a good question," Sam responded. "There are times where the correct financial decision is to partner with an outside firm to provide services that are not your strengths. But, when you bring contractors in, you have to realize your guests usually don't know the difference between contract employees and regular staff. In their eyes, that valet attendant or housekeeper represents the company just as much as the owner or senior manager."

That brought up my next question. "So how do you ensure that contract employees represent your company well?"

Sam cupped his chin between his thumb and forefinger and stroked his neatly trimmed goatee. "You must make sure you have the type of relationship with the partner companies that allows you to hold them to your service standards. I've always insisted that the employees of the partner company participate in some of our training so they understand the culture and the total service picture offered to our guests," Sam explained.

"So tell me about the rest of your scouting mission," Sam said as he refilled my coffee mug.

"We did run into a problem when we attempted to check in to our room. There were four or five stations at the counter, but only one was open. There were about 10 people waiting in line, and it took 25 minutes to get our room keys!" I complained.

"How did you feel at that time?"

"Lisa and I were both irritated," I replied.

"Well, it didn't take you long, but you just hit on the number one customer turnoff: long lines! Let me give you an example," Sam said, rising and moving behind his desk to retrieve a catalog.

"I enjoy shopping at this electronics store," he said, tapping the book he had placed on the desk. "It's a large national chain, and they carry many great products. I can spend hours looking at the TVs, stereos and other gadgets and then go find the less expensive item I need. As I turn the corner to the registers, unfortunately, more often than not, I find a long line of full carts with a small number of registers open. Instantly, that great feeling I had from my shopping experience disappears.

"One time I asked the manager on duty if he could have one of the dozen other employees, who were all just standing around, open a register. Do you know what he said?"

"I bet he said, 'They're not trained to do that job,'" I stuttered.

"You guessed right," Sam laughed. "I take it you've had a similar experience at my electronics store."

"Yes, I have. In fact, I wouldn't do business there if it were the last electronics store in town."

"We're definitely in agreement on that. So now let's move on," Sam said as he sat down and sipped his coffee.

"After we checked in, we headed out to the pool to relax. We had barely set our things down when an attendant appeared to help position our chairs and hand us some towels. He was very polite and took our order for some snacks."

"That sounds pretty good," Sam said.

"It was what happened next that really surprised us. While the attendant was serving our drinks and snacks, he must have overheard us talking about forgetting our sunscreen. It was a lot hotter than we'd expected.

"About two minutes later he returned with a small bottle of sunscreen, enough to take care of our needs for that afternoon... and the best part was that it was complimentary."

"Would you find that at your resort?" Sam asked.

"Unfortunately, I'd have to say 'no,'" I admitted. "But that'll change soon!"

"The rest of the weekend wasn't all that different from our last experience at Fiesta del Sol. There were a few things I found our staff handling better than this resort and a few that made me think about how we needed to improve.

"I did feel our restaurants are superior to Fantasy Vista's in every way," I continued. "It makes me appreciate our head chef. He's the reason our restaurants are so great. I guess he's been taken for granted, but that'll change, too.

"On the other hand, I felt that almost every member of their staff was focused on meeting our needs and making our experience better than we could have imagined. They all appeared to be looking for ways to provide that extra touch during our visit, like that guy at the pool. I noticed this effort all evening, and it made me realize that we need to raise the bar on how we train our staff, how we need to emphasize that each guest deserves that special level of service all the time."

Sam smiled. "You've just discovered the very reason that I encourage everyone to scout their competition! Only good things can happen when you spend some time reviewing how someone else in your industry provides service. During the process, one of two phenomena occurs:

1. You identify some areas where your company provides better service than the competitor, giving you an advantage over your competition. This gives you and your employees a focus on their sense of pride and encourages them to continue delivering this level of service.

2. You spot some service areas where your competitor outshines your own organization. This provides a challenge to improve your service and motivates the employees to try harder to reach this level of service."

Sam then offered an additional thought: "What level or position were the employees that made the experience special?"

"What do you mean?" I responded, not getting his point.

"Just this. People — customers — judge companies based on the people they meet. Sometimes that person could be a voice they hear over the loudspeaker, or it may be the person who answers the telephone," Sam said. "And I'd be willing to bet that the majority of the employees that you interacted with last weekend were not members of the senior leadership team.

"What your experience tells us is that your competitor has met the bigger challenge: to make sure all employees — like the pool attendant — treat their customers with excellent service. And let me add something about lagniappe here. Ever heard of it?"

I hadn't.

Sam went on. "**Lagniappe** (pronounced 'lan-yap') is French for 'a little something extra.' Many years ago in Louisiana, French immigrant merchants used lagniappe as a reward to attract and keep new customers. They had already discovered the key to building customer loyalty.

"For example, if a customer ordered five pounds of sugar, the clerk would dish out five pounds on the scale and then, with a smile, add an additional measure and say, 'Lagniappe.' That was the merchant's way of adding a little extra value and communicating to each customer that 'your business is really important to me.'

"The price of adding that extra measure may have already been backed into the price of five pounds of sugar, but the return on whatever the investment may be is worth much more than anything else the merchant could have done to thank each customer."

"I see what you're saying," I nodded. "But since I'm not going to be able to be with every guest, how do you ensure that your standards, such as offering lagniappe, are practiced by all your employees?"

"It's called accountability, and we'll talk about it next week."

"Sounds good," I said, "and that leads me to my next question, Sam. What do you recommend if you don't have a local company in town that is also a competitor?"

"Sometimes you won't find a direct competitor to observe,"

Sam responded. "In those cases, you may have to be a bit creative and look at service examples in similar organizations. You can even look at other divisions or departments in your own company. Sometimes it works well to meet with your peers in other departments and share your best practices. They may be doing something creative that you could adapt to your staff.

"There's a philosophy in leadership that says, 'The trailing edge prospers,' Sam continued. "It means that you don't always have to invent everything you do. Sometimes it works to your advantage to take things that have already been invented and do them better. Companies often miss the best opportunities by not looking internally."

That made sense — and it made me think about how the ideas we had incorporated in the accounting department could easily translate into the customer service area.

"I have another easy way to stay current with what your competitors are doing," Sam said. "Almost every industry has one or more major trade shows each year. I always tried to attend at least one, depending on time and resources. This allowed me to interact with my vendors and partners, but more importantly, I spent informal time with my peers in competing organizations," he explained.

"Trade shows? Because of my role in the company, I never took the time to participate in them," I responded. "Part of the drawback was the expense of those events, along with the time it took away from the office."

"That's how many people feel, but I usually come back from

conventions and conferences with a lot of fresh ideas, new relationships with others in my industry, and enthusiasm about incorporating what I've learned. For some reason, people who would be very hesitant to share information about their operation under normal circumstances tend to be more willing to talk when they're out of the office and in enjoyable surroundings."

I nodded my head in agreement. That also made sense.

Sam continued. "Most of the conferences bring in great speakers, and you gain a lot of knowledge in a short length of time. The exposition area — where vendors who specialize in your field can demonstrate their latest products and services — is worth the price of admission in itself. If you happen to be in the market for something like a new software package, a conference can be the best place to see several options before you make a decision."

"Do you have any recommendations for good conventions in the hospitality industry?" I asked.

"I'll pull some information from my files and send it to you this week. I think there's a good event coming up in the next few months," Sam replied, standing up and stretching his full 6-foot 2-inch frame. "Well, we'd better call it a morning. Have a great week, and I'll see you back next Monday."

"You must have an important golf outing planned," I joked.

"Why do you say that?" Sam asked.

"You almost let me get away without summarizing the main points from our session!" I replied.

"You're right!" Sam took his seat and motioned for me to begin.

"Looking over my notes, I placed an asterisk by these points:

1. The number one customer turnoff is long lines. I need to minimize the time our customers are waiting for an attraction or some other service.

2. Scouting the competition results in one of two responses:
   - We will have pride in our work because we were better than the competition.
   - We will strive to improve in an area to reach and surpass our competition.

3. "Lagniappe" — always give the customer a little extra.

4. The trailing edge prospers. You don't always have to be the first to do something. Capitalize on the other guy's hard work and improve on it.

5. Trade shows can be an efficient way to scout your competition and come up with new ideas."

"I think you got the main points. I'm glad you caught me before you headed out the door and I took off for the course," Sam laughed. "I'll see you next Monday."

The Third Monday

Chisel A Culture of Accountability

It was hard to believe that it was already time for my third meeting with Sam. With only one week remaining before I assumed the director of Guest Services position, my time with Sam was more valuable than ever.

It was a perfect Monday morning, and I arrived at the beach house right on time. Seagulls were following the shrimpers out into the bay, and their cries added just the right tone to this bright, clear morning.

"Well, we're making a habit of this Monday morning thing, aren't we, Brett?" Sam laughed as I shook his hand at the door and followed him to the expansive deck at the back of his home. I found a chaise and sat back, watching the rolling surf as it wiped the beach clean of footprints and pawprints left by a trio that had just strolled by.

"I'm so thankful that you've been willing to give me so much of your time," I began. "If I had to pay for your guidance and your insights, I'd have had to get a second mortgage."

"No problem. An old retired guy can't golf every day." As usual, Sam had a hot mug of coffee ready, and we settled in for our third week of customer service mentoring.

"As we finished up last week, you seemed to be grappling with the realization that you will not be able to be with every customer every day." Sam commented.

"Yes, that's true," I said. "And I'm still dealing with the question of how you ensure that your staff members are performing up to your standards and delivering lagniappe."

"It's all about accountability," Sam replied easily. "You have to establish processes that help you and your leadership team hold each other and the frontline staff accountable for every minute of their performance.

"Much like a sculptor, your job is to take this piece of marble — your entire team — and chisel a culture of accountability. It takes time and crafting, but it is possible," Sam assured. "And let me add this one other comment about molding your team — don't think it will always be easy. So this accountability thing requires effort, innovation and often just hanging in there until it comes together. Remember that a diamond is a chunk of coal that made good under pressure."

"Can you give me some specifics?" I was curious. Sam seemed to make everything so easily obvious.

"Sure. I have a formula for success." He held up a sheet of paper. "It goes like this:

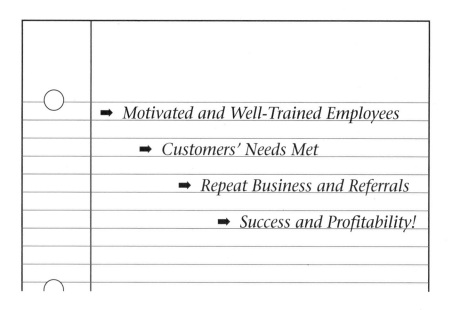

> ➡ *Motivated and Well-Trained Employees*
>
> ➡ *Customers' Needs Met*
>
> ➡ *Repeat Business and Referrals*
>
> ➡ *Success and Profitability!*

"As you notice, it all starts with the employees, primarily the frontline workers who have the most interaction with your customers. You can spend a lot of energy ensuring that your leadership team is trained and that you have correct policies, which is important, but it will be a waste of money if your frontline employees are not motivated, incented and trained to implement the policies designed to satisfy your customers.

"And it all starts with your orientation program for new employees. Many companies have turned this into a human resources session where the main goal is filling out forms to get insurance and benefits. Sure, this is important and needs to happen, but orientation should not stop once the forms are completed and the insurance coverage is selected."

I could see that Sam was just getting started. I furiously took notes as he spoke.

"There are three important aspects of any initial training program:

1. **Culture.** All employees (and critical contractors) should know the history and values that shape your company. This includes setting expectations on how your customers are to be treated. Your employees' knowledge of corporate culture will help shape their work values, their work ethic and their ability to fit in, continue and probably improve the culture that's in place. In fact, in most corporations, the culture is the mechanism that creates the work ethic for most employees.

2. **Job Training.** All employees should know the details of their assigned jobs and should be able to carry out their duties effectively. The number one reason people don't do what they're supposed to do in their jobs is because they don't know what they're supposed to do. Here's an example: In one corporation where I was asked to consult, the employees had been through orientation and were told that the corporate leadership expected all employees to be involved in the community. Some of the employees perceived that this meant that every spare minute away from the office should be spent being active in the community. In fact, several employees even took vacation days to facilitate their community involvement. That, of course, was a noble thing, but sooner or later those employees began resenting that so much of their free time was being devoted to civic activities.

They perceived one thing, and the corporation's expectations were entirely different. In that corporate culture, twice a year, the entire company took one day to do something for the community — build a playground, wrap presents for homeless kids or participate in other community outreach programs. There was no demand to take vacation days for community involvement — which was the employees' perception, but it didn't match the employer's expectation.

In terms of work, management emphasized exceeding sales quotas. New employees saw a big chance to gain instant credibility by going out and getting new customers. In doing so, they paid little attention to established customers — and this inattention led to some of the firm's loyal customers abandoning ship for the competition. The new employees scored points — even got extra bonus money for recruiting new customers. Being rewarded for their activities, the new employees continued to ignore established customers — and when they were eventually questioned about their productivity, the employees became confused about exactly what management expected.

3. **Cross-training.** Each employee at any level in the organization, including your receptionist or valet attendant, should know the key services and products that your company offers to clients.

Not only does this equip them with an ability to fill in staffing gaps, but it also gives them some idea of the big picture...and there are several other benefits. As you cross-train people, learning other jobs and how they work gives them some idea of how what they do on a daily basis impacts the next person in line and then how the big picture — what everybody does impacts the customer.

Cross-training gives individual team members the ability to see what impact they personally make on the big picture, i.e., the customer, and it also gives them an opportunity to explore personal skill sets in various areas, which often makes it possible for employees and managers to make better decisions about career-path issues.

Finally, a cross-trained staff always has a better idea of what it takes to keep sharp and to provide the very best customer service because they know how the 'machine' works and what's possible in a variety of situations."

He stopped for a sip of coffee and patted his mouth quickly with a napkin.

I had always been a supporter of training, but I was not seeing the connection between training and accountability. "Sam, help me out with the big picture."

"What's the first thing you would hear from an employee if you confront them about a service delivery issue?" Sam asked.

"Well, I usually hear, 'I haven't been trained in that area,'" I responded.

"Correct. If an employee isn't confident about performing their job and unable to answer basic questions that a customer may pose to them, they will not be as effective with your customers as they could be," Sam pointed out, taking another sip of his coffee and then continuing.

"Once someone has a good grasp on the execution of their job, they can relax and focus on adding those 'extras' you noticed when you spent the night at your competitor's resort. Once the employer satisfies their part of the bargain — training the employee, providing recognition and positive incentives, plus using clear-cut policies and specific expectations — then the company is justified in expecting their employees to deliver extraordinary customer service.

"Now back to the issue of accountability." Sam was on a roll and was obviously enjoying himself. "It's important that your customers have the ability to offer positive or constructive feedback about your staff and services. And it's even more important that you develop an internal process to handle this information."

"Okay, I hear you. So how would you suggest dealing with feedback about an employee who is accused of rude treatment or poor customer service?" I asked.

"One of the best parts of having a process to analyze feedback is that it lets you spot trends and identify employees or processes that may require some corrective action. This allows you to avoid coming down on every employee for every failure. People will make mistakes," Sam replied. "It's human nature and definitely part of doing business."

"I worked with one of our subsidiary companies, Harris

Relocations, a few years back," I offered. "They had a Client Relations' phone number where clients or others who depended on our services could call if they weren't receiving the service they expected. This group would handle the calls one at a time and try to resolve the specific complaint."

"That sounds okay," Sam continued. "But the problem is, they weren't looking at the data in total in order to spot trends at certain locations or problems with particular employees. They also were not bringing these issues to the attention of the leadership team. A few years before I retired, we started a new process where the Executive Leadership Team reviewed a report in their weekly team meeting that contained a summary and the details of each complaint call. They were broken down by area of responsibility. Each executive reviewed the report dealing with their area of responsibility and had until the next meeting to determine why the problem had occurred. In some cases, they required the frontline employee to write a letter of apology to the customer."

"That sounds great. What were the results?" I inquired.

"We had one troubling area regarding the prompt return of phone calls. After just one week of using this accountability process, the number of this type of complaint went down 30 percent!" Sam was enthusiastic about the results — his eyes sparkled as he enjoyed thinking back on the days when he was active in his business.

"Wow. I guess the staff realized they were being watched, and they started doing the right thing," I surmised.

"You're right, but in most cases, what it all comes down to is that what you pay attention to gets done," Sam said.

"Well, this sounds fine, but how do you implement accountability processes without creating the fear among your employees of Big Brother watching every move?" I asked.

"Good question," Sam replied as he refreshed both of our mugs. "Most employees are trying to do a good job. In many cases, employees — at all levels — realize that their reputation is tied to the performance of their co-workers as well as their own. I've found that the ones that are doing a good job appreciate it when leadership deals with the poor performers," Sam pointed out.

That made sense. Even I had found myself concerned when a co-worker didn't finish a project on time, because it made the rest of the group look bad — and I was glad when upper management either moved that employee to a less-demanding job or terminated him or her because of consistently poor performance.

"I've also found another common theme in many of the organizations," Sam said.

"What's that?" I wondered.

"Many times an organization has the best intentions to make improvements in customer service or in their products. What I find is that leadership tends to analyze plans to death and rarely implements most of them. This frustrates your customers as well as your employees," my mentor explained.

"That's also true in our company," I said "So what did you do to solve this problem?"

"Well, let's start with first things first. We initiated a process with my leadership team that created an expectation of regular progress on each major objective of the improvement plan. At the core of this process is a simple document that lists the major issues being faced by the organization. For each issue, we then identify a point person, a member of our team who has the responsibility for implementing that particular plan. The document also contains an eventual goal for each issue and a short description of the status," Sam explained.

"But the key is in this next item," he continued. "For each issue, we're forced to come up with a milestone or significant accomplishment, to be completed in the next two to four weeks, that will move us closer to the goal."

"I've done similar things before," I mentioned. "What I've found is that the deadlines come and go, and we simply adjust the goal dates."

"That's what most organizations do," Sam nodded in agreement. "To avoid that problem, I held a weekly leadership team meeting. The first thing we did during each meeting was review our progress on each issue. The point person would give an update and explain why any target was missed. Missing targets soon became uncomfortable to explain to the rest of us, so after a few weeks, I noticed that nearly everyone had met his or her two- to four-week goals. The end result was that we started implementing solutions instead of just talking about them."

"I'm going to give this a try," I decided on the spot. "Do you have a template of the document I could use to get started?"

"Sure. I'll e-mail it to you later today," Sam responded, then added, "Now I want to change direction on this topic. Let me ask you a question."

"Shoot."

"What do you typically do when you identify a member of your staff who consistently does an excellent job with what you give them?" Sam's smile indicated he already knew the answer.

"Well, I guess I'd give them more work," I responded.

"And what do you do when someone is not delivering as you expect?" Sam questioned again.

"I take work away from them and give it to the ones who are performing," I replied.

"Do you see a problem with this pattern?"

"Sure. It rewards poor performance and doesn't give someone much of an incentive to be a star performer, does it?" I replied as if a light were simultaneously flashing before me.

"No, it doesn't. So what we have to learn to do is to deal with the poor performers through coaching, discipline or termination. Many leaders feel that 'a warm body in this role is better than no one,' but I tend to disagree. Having the wrong person in a role or holding on to a poor performer because you don't want to go through the hassle of hiring someone will cost you in the end and at the bottom line."

Sam continued after confirming that I understood his concept. "I also noticed another trend in several of our companies a few years back. After identifying a problem with a staff member through the accountability reports, I would discuss it with their leadership and others who knew the person. What I typically heard was, 'I'm not surprised. We've had problems with that person for years.' So do you know what I'd do next?" he asked, not waiting for my response.

"I also took a look at their past performance reviews, and guess what I'd find in most of the cases."

"Let me guess," I began. "Probably glowing reports with no mention of the problem area. I've been guilty of this same practice in the past," I confessed.

"Right on. Many managers seem to have a problem giving what I call a 'balanced' review," Sam pointed out. "We owe it to the employees to let them know when they are not meeting our expectations. This is done through timely informal discussions as well as the written review process. Most employees will make an attempt to correct a problem if they know about it — if you let them know about it."

"In our company, we have a review process, but it's very complex, and the leaders all dread the review time of year. In fact, some of my peers actually try to skip the process — and get away with it until the employee badgers them enough to get it done. What do you suggest?" I asked.

"I use the following principle:

> *It is more important that an employee receive timely,*
> *balanced feedback than using any type of*
> *fancy sophisticated tool.*
> *My rule is — Keep it SIMPLE!*

I recommended to all my area managers that they use a simple three-part review form:

1. **Positive Feedback.** What did the employee do that was excellent or above your expectations?

2. **Constructive Feedback.** What should the employee improve, start doing or stop doing?

3. **Job-Specific Goals.** Develop in advance four to five goals with specific measurements and record whether the employee met the goal, did not meet the goal or partially met the goal."

"How often should you perform formal reviews?" I inquired.

"I recommend going through this process every six months with all employees and every three months during an employee's first year. Any less frequently, and it's not effective, and any more frequently, you feel that you're always conducting reviews," Sam answered.

We both sat in silence for several moments, mentally reviewing our discussion. Then Sam spoke. "Well, I think that's enough for today. Why don't you tell me the main points that we discussed this morning?"

"Wow. We covered a lot today. Let me think.

1. The first step toward accountability is to fulfill your responsibilities as an employer to properly train each employee.

2. Create a process to analyze customer feedback to spot trends and take action.

3. Don't be afraid to discipline and terminate employees who are not performing. The good employees will appreciate it when you hold everyone accountable.

4. Conduct regular balanced reviews, and keep the process simple."

Sam added, "And don't forget, it's only through setting clear expectations and then holding everyone accountable that you will be able to ensure your standards are being met as they relate to the treatment of your customers."

I stood and shook Sam's hand as we moved back into the house.

"Once again, I have a lot to think about this week. I'll do a little homework and find out about the accountability processes that have been in place in this department. Thanks again. This is really helping me prepare for my new job!"

"No problem. I look forward to our meetings also. See you next Monday," Sam replied.

The Fourth Monday

Know Your Stuff

It was hard for me to believe that I would be starting my new job later that day as I drove south to Sam's for our fourth meeting. I was a little edgy this trip, eager to learn more and wanting to spend as much time as possible with Sam, but equally excited about meeting my new staff and starting to apply some of what I had learned thus far.

I also was looking forward to my Monday morning with Sam even more because he had provided so much information to make my transition much less foreboding.

I had spent some time the previous week looking into our company's accountability processes. As Sam had mentioned, Harris Hospitality had an incomplete process for gathering customer feedback. We collected the information from internal comment cards and tabulated the data, but the process stopped there.

The leaders responsible for the various areas mentioned in the comment cards had never been held accountable for identifying the source of the problem, nor had they taken the next step — finding out how to prevent the problem from occurring in the future.

My head was spinning with questions for Sam as I approached his house. I was surprised to find Sam's wife, Becky, waiting at the door.

"Come in, Brett," Becky said warmly as she gave me a hug. "Sam is tied up on a phone call and asked me to greet you. He'll be with you shortly. May I get you some coffee?"

"Yes, thank you. I sure appreciate you letting me borrow Sam for these Monday mornings. I don't know what I'd do without his help and wisdom."

"Truthfully, I think Sam looks forward to these sessions as much as, or more, than you! It gives him an opportunity to share his experiences, and it keeps him from spending time hunting down his golf balls," Becky laughed.

"What's so funny out here?" boomed Sam as he appeared to join us on the deck.

"Oh, nothing, honey," Becky said with a wink as she returned to the house.

"Let's get down to business," Sam began. "Sorry I'm late. So how was your week, Brett?"

"It was interesting," I said. "I did a bit of homework and confirmed what you said last week about most companies and their accountability processes. We definitely have some work to do!"

"Our feedback loop is more of a semicircle, and our employee review process is more of an exercise than a tool to help prepare our staff for delivering excellent service," I responded.

"Let me know if you need some more help in this area." Sam obviously had more experience in closing the loop than I.

"I appreciate that. I think I have a plan for making some changes, thanks to you."

"Well, then, let's get down to today's topic." I could see Sam was anxious to cover some ground.

"What's the topic?" I queried. "I realized after I left last week that you hadn't told me what our session was going to be about today."

"You're right. I decided you had enough to think about last week," Sam said, "so today we're going to talk about the importance of knowing your product or service, or as I sometimes refer to it, 'knowing your stuff' — for management as well as employees."

"Sounds interesting."

"Let me tell you about an experience I had a few years ago to illustrate the first point I want to make," Sam started out. "I was in the market for a new car, and Becky and I were looking at a minivan to cart our grandkids around in. I'd done my research and found a particular vehicle from Honda that had some innovative features. I drove to the dealership a few miles from our home. As I got out of my car, I noticed a salesperson standing around at the showroom door.

"He waited at the entrance until Becky and I reached the front doors of the dealership.

"'Hello, my name is Cal,' he said, extending his hand to both of us. 'Which car can I put you in today?' Cal had memorized a typical sales intro.

"I told Cal that I was interested in their new minivan. He pointed to several of the vehicles halfway across the lot and said he would be happy to show me the cars. We got to the minivan he had in mind, and guess what happened?"

"I don't know. What?" I questioned.

"Cal wrote down a number off the vehicle and said politely, 'Let me go get a key. I'll be right back.'"

"I failed to mention that this was in August, and it was 98 degrees in the shade," Sam continued. "He disappeared for five to ten minutes and then showed up with the key. Now, I know you aren't a car salesperson, but, Brett, what would have been the better way of handling this situation?" Sam asked.

"Cal should have known the vehicle number and retrieved the key before walking to the minivan in the heat," I answered.

"Right. That may require a change in their process to keep a list of vehicles and their key numbers with the salesperson. The bad thing is that this salesperson didn't have a clue that there was anything wrong," Sam responded. "In my book, the best companies are the ones who are always looking out for the interests of their customers. But wait. It gets better!" Sam smiled, and I knew there was a good story coming.

"One of the new features in this minivan that had made me

curious was a new third seat that folded down and disappeared into the cargo area, leaving a lot of room for bags, luggage or my golf clubs.

"I asked Cal to show me how this worked, even though I had read all about it on the Internet. Well, poor Cal spent the next five minutes trying to find the release button that allowed the seat to fold and store. I watched as we all sweated in the heat. After five minutes, I offered my assistance and spent the next 15 minutes showing Cal how it worked."

"Did you buy the car?" I asked.

"Yes, but not from that dealership. I drove 30 minutes across town and found a dealership where the salesperson knew more about the car than I did. The easy lesson here is that Cal should have spent some time early on familiarizing himself with the features of the cars he sold instead of standing around waiting on someone to drive up. His lack of knowledge, courtesy and common sense cost him the sale," Sam explained.

"Now, let me give you another example. Have you ever called a business and tried to ask the receptionist a basic question and were told, 'I'm just the receptionist. I don't know the answer to your question.'"

"Sure," I said. "It happened the other day, and I was just trying to find out if Extreme Video, an audiovisual company, sold projection screens. The receptionist was polite, but clueless!"

"This goes back to what we talked about during our discussion on accountability," Sam continued. "It's important that each employee is highly trained in his or her area of expertise, but it is equally important for him or her to have a base level of knowledge in other areas within your company."

"How does anyone know enough to answer any and every question a guest may ask?" I wondered aloud.

"That's a good point. They're not expected to answer every question, but they should at least know the basic services and products available through your organization. At a minimum, they should know who to call and where to direct the customer who has asked the question." Sam sounded like this was one of his passions within the realm of customer service.

"That makes sense," I decided. "I guess that's where cross-training comes into play."

"You're exactly right." Sam beamed at my response. "I encourage all staff members to take a few hours each month to shadow, or watch over the shoulder of, another team member from a different area. Quite often it helps both employees gain a better understanding of the client's needs and how they can satisfy them."

"I have one more benefit of cross training your staff and leaders I want to share," Sam said, taking another long sip of his coffee.

"Have you ever had a situation in one of your departments where you were critically short of staff or leadership due to an unexpected resignation or other departure?" he asked.

"Yes. Several years ago we had a payroll manager, Donna, who was involved in a serious car accident. She recovered but was out of work for six weeks. We quickly realized that she was the only one in the entire organization who knew how to enter the financial data into our computer system. We had to process our payroll manually for two pay periods. We got through it, but it put a strain on our entire group." I explained.

"Exactly. If you spend some time cross-training employees in key positions, you'll be better prepared for situations like the one you just described. When I start in a new position, one of the first things I do is look over the organization and try to identify any single points of failure or positions that do not have a backup individual or process.

"Let me give you another example." Sam's examples made his lessons indelible in my mind. He was a superb teacher.

"I was visiting a theme park attraction with Becky and two of our grandchildren a few years ago, and I asked the person taking the tickets to tell me about her three favorite attractions. Our time was limited, and I wanted to make the best of our visit. The employee's response surprised me. The young lady told us that she had only visited one-third of the attractions. I expected to find that she was new in her position, but when I asked her how long she'd worked there, she told me she'd been there seven years."

Sam continued. "If I were running that operation, every employee would be required to sample each attraction as part of his or her orientation. This experience would allow them to provide better advice to the guests, and they would also be better equipped to provide suggestions to improve a particular attraction or the service available at that attraction."

I could see his point: time invested at the front end would pay off down the line. "I'll have to look into our practice in this area," I said. "If I were a betting man, I'd wager that we train new staff members only in their assigned areas."

"I've seen this done as a fun exercise during training," Sam pointed out. "The person conducting the orientation class would hand out a Know Your Company game. The new employees would pair up and have a set amount of time to determine the answers to common questions that a customer may ask. Some of the answers could be found only by experiencing some of the attractions. To complete other questions, you would have to speak with an employee from that area. The group would then get back together and compare answers, with the winner receiving a prize."

"Sounds like fun," I agreed.

"One more thought," Sam offered. "I've rotated my leaders to different positions within the organization. It may be intimidating at first, but I've found it prevents them from becoming stagnant in their positions, and they often bring fresh ideas to their new position that truly benefits our customers."

"I can relate to that idea!" I laughed.

Sam had one more thought on this topic. "I was working with one organization several years ago that had six different departments, similar to how your organization is set up. They each delivered different services to the customers. In many instances, a single customer would receive more than one service from our company. Based on some feedback from our customers, it became obvious that many of our employees did not know what the other departments did."

"What solution did you recommend?"

"Well, we first created a small team that developed Quick Reference Fact Sheets for each of the six departments," Sam said. "These color-coded handouts included a single sheet for each department that described the most important facts for their area. It also included important phone numbers if they needed more information to assist a customer."

"I bet most of our team members wouldn't be able to answer simple questions about one of the other departments," I said. "I may look into doing something like this."

"Sounds like a plan, but before you get busy with that new job, why don't you make sure you have all the concepts down from today's discussion?" Sam suggested.

"This was an easy topic for me. This all makes sense. Here are the main points:

1. Make sure all employees are trained and can answer a customer's questions about their area of expertise. If a customer does not feel that the employee knows what they are talking about, they will go elsewhere to find employees who are knowledgeable — and they'll have more confidence in that company or their products.

2. Cross-train all staff members. Every employee should know the basics about products, services and whom to call to get more information for a customer. This process also creates a backup person for each critical process.

3. Create Quick Reference Fact Sheets to help every employee understand what each department does and whom to call for more information.

4. Rotate your leaders to different areas. This will help them keep fresh, gain new ideas and uncover problems that may not be found otherwise."

Sam nodded approvingly. "I think you're ready to get some real-life practice in your new position, but before you go, I want to add something about that last point. We once moved our leaders around and found that one well-thought-of executive had been suppressing a lot of negative customer feedback. He was ignoring frequent guest complaints about a particular employee. The employee happened to be a personal friend, and the manager was trying to protect his friend's job. We would never have known this situation existed if a new leader had not been given responsibility for this area."

"So, Sam, what are we going to talk about next week?" I inquired as I picked up my notes and prepared to leave.

"We're going to discuss the difference between 'onstage' and 'backstage,'" Sam responded. "This is one of my favorite topics and something that can make the difference between an average and outstanding experience for your guests."

"Wish me well," I said as I walked with Sam toward the door. "I'm reporting to my new office as soon as I leave here. I have a feeling I'll be needing an extended session next week."

"You'll do fine," Sam encouraged, patting me on the back. "You have plenty to work on in your first few weeks. I always say you can measure the quality of a leader by what they accomplish in their first 120 days on a new job."

"See you next Monday," I said as I waved goodbye to Becky, who was looking through the kitchen window.

"Same time, same place," Sam responded. "Time to go hit a few white balls around and work on my self-control."

Keep Backstage
Things Backstage

I t had been a long week! I had spent most of my time this first week in my new job getting to know my staff members and reviewing processes and procedures impacting customer service. I felt like I had 10 times more questions than answers as I navigated my way.

I woke up extra early and arrived at Sam's 30 minutes before our scheduled time. I decided to wait in my car in the driveway, but Sam saw me and motioned me inside.

"I figured you might get here a little early. Come on in," Sam said with a grin.

We went through our routine of filling our mugs with coffee and retiring to the deck in the comfortable patio chairs. The morning sun was just beginning to glint off the waves. We sat in silence, taking in Nature's panorama before we began our meeting.

"I'm going to have to get used to making my own coffee again when we complete our time together!" I joked.

"Well, so tell me. How was your first week on the new job?" Sam asked eagerly. "Any war stories?"

"It was a bit intense," I admitted. "I spent a lot of time in meetings with the CEO, which were enlightening, but they also kept me from doing some of what I had planned to do in my first few days on the job. I also spent a lot of time looking at our properties, which also ate up a lot of the time I had planned to spend with my team.

"Eventually, I made room in this hectic schedule to go around and introduce myself to my new team members. It will take some time to be able to match names with duties, but we were able to have a couple of meetings to establish communication, which I think were useful. We also had time to meet socially for a dinner so we could get some idea of how we were going to match, personality-wise, as we set out on this grand adventure," I quipped. "But really, even though it was a fast week and a tough week, it was also gratifying from a lot of perspectives... and it made me realize that these next few meetings, as well as our first meetings, were even more valuable than I'd first envisioned."

"Sounds like you've found yourself some real challenges, Brett, so let's get on to our topic for today." Sam seemed excited about our pending discussion.

"Do you have an idea of what I'm talking about when I say onstage and backstage?" he asked.

"I guess onstage means activity in front of your guests or customers, and backstage is when you are only with your employees," I replied.

"That's right!" Sam said. "Let me give you an example. Early in my career I was in a sales position for a growing company and took a potential client on a tour of our office. They would've been one of our largest clients and would have made for a nice Christmas for my family if I could've brought them on board! We had a call center in a corner of the office area, and I wanted to show the potential client this impressive area. As we walked around the corner, we saw two of our younger employees taking a break, and we heard them talking about one of our existing clients."

"I can smell this one coming," I smiled.

"These staff members were making some very unprofessional statements about this client," Sam continued, "and even discussed his financial holdings with our company. My potential client heard every word. I tried to move him on to a different area, but the damage was done. He was polite and acted as if he had not heard this embarrassing conversation, but he never became a client."

"I bet it wasn't a good day for those two employees!" I chuckled.

"No, it wasn't. They got their one warning," Sam replied.

"Did you encounter any examples of backstage activities being conducted onstage that day you took your friends to Fiesta del Sol?" Sam asked.

"Yeah, several," I remembered. "We had spent a lot of money (and I know because I prepared the checks) to create a new themed area in the park. The landscaping, architecture and costumes were all from a time period 2,000 years ago. You actually started to feel that you were going back to that time as you walked through the front gate and around the first corner."

"So what happened?" Sam asked.

"I turned the corner and found myself (and my guests) looking at a trash dumpster and some broken-down equipment. The large gate had been opened, and by the looks of the tracks on the ground, it stayed in that position most of the time.

"I asked one of the employees in the area why the gate was open, and he replied, 'It's always has been like that. I guess someone got tired of opening it and closing it again, so they decided to leave it open all the time.'"

"Sometimes it requires more work to present that top-notch onstage experience for your guests." Sam nodded knowingly. "But, of course, it's always easier to take a shortcut."

"So how do you maintain that excellent presentation for guests? I'd bet that when people work at a job for a long time, it's easy to overlook those seemingly unimportant details. It wouldn't take long to get used to seeing the garbage dumpster and not think anything of it."

Sam was ready with an answer, as I knew he would be. "That's where you and your managers come in. You must resist the temptation to stay buried in your office, completing paperwork or handling personnel issues. It's imperative that you spend some time each day walking the property and observing the various guest areas," Sam replied.

"The director of Guest Services must be the 'champion' for

every customer," he went on. "Part of your responsibility is to monitor your services and environment to make sure your staff doesn't accept things like we've discussed today. Dumpsters and service equipment onstage put your park in a bad light, particularly when they interfere with a guest's experience, so you should also be the one who makes sure all your employees are trained in this important area of customer service.

"Remember this — great customer service skills are like air in an old bicycle tire…it leaks. So how do you plug the leak? First, you must continuously remind your staff that excellent customer service is key to your success," Sam said passionately. "Leading by example is another way to plug that leak — and don't forget to give your employees the opportunity to learn new skills and reinforce their existing ones."

"Do you have another example of improper backstage activities that sometimes make their way onstage," I asked, "maybe one that would relate to our hotel operations?"

"Sure. I went to a hotel in San Francisco just a few weeks ago," Sam began, being the marvelous storyteller he was. "I was out there attending a publisher's convention, and Becky and I had taken a few extra days to do some sightseeing. During the last night of the conference, the group sponsored a nice dinner in one of the downtown hotel ballrooms. Everything was well done, including the table decorations. The food was outstanding, and they had one of my favorite desserts!"

"What's your favorite dessert?" I interjected curiously.

"It was a chocolate mousse dessert with white, milk, and dark chocolate in the shape of a lighthouse. I ate mine and the one at the empty seat next to us while the lights were down for the presentation," Sam confessed.

"I'm also curious about why you were at a publisher's convention," I said.

"Becky is interested in writing a book about her experiences as the daughter of a missionary. I'm going to help her with the editing," Sam explained, "but back to my story. During the time the dinner was being served, the hotel staff left the door to the kitchen wide open. Not only could we see all the preparation activities, but the kitchen staff made quite a racket. It goes without saying...everyone in that ballroom was drawn to that noisy kitchen with all its clanging and banging instead of toward the poor speaker up front who was trying to capture the audience's attention."

"What would you recommend in that instance?" I asked.

"Most upscale hotels have portable dividers they decorate and place in front of the doors to the kitchen. They also make sure they train their kitchen staff to keep a check on their noise level," Sam explained.

"I'll check on that when I get back to the office today," I promised.

Sam continued. "Over the years, I've also used another tool to keep us from overlooking backstage issues. It's called a Mystery Guest service. I had a contract with an independent company to visit our facility at random periods several times a year. They would look and act like a guest. No one, including myself, knew who this person would be or when he or she would come. They would spend the day at one of our facilities and interact with our staff, throwing a curve ball now and then to see how they would respond," he explained.

"Did they give you a report card after they visited your site?" I asked.

"Yes. They would meet with my entire leadership team and discuss their findings. They would point out excellent service as well as areas that needed some attention," Sam continued. "Sometimes their report was embarrassingly honest. Other times, I was genuinely pleased with what they found."

"Did they identify things that even you missed?"

"You bet. I've found that an outsider tends to ask the tough questions and notices things that have become commonplace to my entire team," Sam answered. "I'd encourage you to engage a similar company or find someone from another division who would be willing to work with you in this capacity. If you need the name of the group I used, I'd be happy to get that for you."

"Sure I'd be interested," I said eagerly. "It sounds like a valuable and worthwhile service."

I looked at my watch. "Well, I better get going. I have a meeting with my leadership team after lunch, but before I leave, I suppose you want me to summarize what I learned," I said.

"You got it. You didn't think I'd let you off easy, did you?" Sam laughed.

"Okay. These are the main points from today's session:

1. 'Onstage' means things that the customer is supposed to hear or see.

2. 'Backstage' means things that should be done behind the scenes where the customer does not hear or see them.

3. Employees should always be trained to respect the customer...no matter what the situation.

4. My ultimate job is to maintain a high standard of service and ensure that backstage activities are truly behind the scene.

5. Use a Mystery Guest service to provide a fresh look at our environment and service quality."

"That sounds right," Sam replied. "And don't forget, the organizations at the top of their industry are the ones that understand and practice the onstage versus backstage principles."

"Got it. So what's on the agenda for next week?" I asked eagerly.

"We're going to discuss the importance of utilizing your entire team to serve your customers," Sam responded. "And, by the way, have a great meeting this afternoon."

"I'll let you know how it goes. Thanks again for everything," I replied. "See you next Monday!"

Get Off Your Island!

This past week had been one of the busiest I could remember. Every time I felt that I understood an aspect of my new job, I uncovered five more that I did not have a clue about. I spent most of the weekend at the office, trying to catch up and get ready for the next week. Sunday night I was feeling the pressure and called Sam to see if we could skip our meeting the next morning.

"Hello. This is Sam."

"Hey, Sam. This is Brett."

"Well, hello, Brett. Couldn't wait until tomorrow?" Sam laughed.

"Actually, I called to see if we could skip our session this week. I've had a crazy week, and I don't think I have the time to spend on our session. I have so many due dates and things to learn, I need every minute," I explained.

Sam sighed. "I figured this day would come. Actually, I was expecting a call last week."

I could tell Sam was disappointed.

"Brett, you're falling into the habits that most people in the working world develop when things get tough," Sam continued.

"What do you mean, Sam?"

"The majority of people tend to operate in a reactionary mode, responding to the emergency of the day," Sam explained. "Once a person gets into this mode and stops taking regular time to plan, train and prepare for their week, it's very hard to ever reclaim the time to be proactive.

"Brett, I strongly encourage you to keep our appointment for tomorrow," said Sam in an insistent tone. "Those projects and issues will be there when you get to your office. And let me say just one other thing about this. The most effective people I've ever known aggressively defend their planning and self-improvement time. They've learned they can accomplish much more if they're organized and prepared to face each week. I strongly urge you to take that time away from the urgencies of the day and spend some time improving your skills and planning for your future tasks and projects," Sam concluded.

After that discussion, how could I not show up on Monday? "Okay, Sam. I see your point. Look for me tomorrow at 8:00 a.m. sharp. I do value our time together. It's just that I was feeling overwhelmed," I explained.

"No problem. See you in the morning. I'll make extra-strong coffee!" Sam laughed.

I felt bad for trying to cancel my meeting, but I knew Sam

understood my feelings.

The next morning I was actually looking forward to my time with Sam. I went into the office early before heading across town to the beach house.

"Hi, Brett," Sam called out as I walked up the sidewalk. "I'm glad you made it."

"Good morning, Sam. Sorry about that call last night," I apologized. "I hope you weren't offended."

"No offense taken. It's a natural reaction when things get tough," Sam responded. "Here's your coffee. Now let's get down to business so you can get back to your office on time."

We sat and sipped as we watched the waves play across the sandy beach, each one reaching farther inland as the tide rose.

"So how did your meeting go last week?" Sam asked as we settled into our usual chairs.

"Well, that's actually when my anxiety started. I guess the first week was my honeymoon in the new job. During this meeting I learned of no less than five significant problem areas I would be expected to solve," I replied. "My directors all seemed to be concerned only with their own areas, which brings up my first question — how do you get them to function as a team?"

"That'll take some time, but don't give up hope. It can happen," Sam said reassuringly. "Whenever I was given responsibility for a new department during my career, my first objective was to get my executive leadership team to expand their interests and participation beyond their individual departments.

"The senior leaders should have the best interest of the entire organization at heart. We started working as a team when my leaders began helping each other solve problems and volunteered to move resources to the major point of need," Sam explained.

"That sounds great, but how do I get them to start helping each other?" I asked, concerned that it was sounding like I was asking for a magic wand.

"The first thing I do is to have them spend some time understanding the other departments and their critical issues and needs. I also ask for volunteers and make assignments to solve problems, using executives from several areas, not just the executive responsible for the problem area," Sam continued. "Let me give you a few examples to illustrate the importance of team service."

"Sure. I'd like to hear them."

"One of my favorite restaurants in Orlando does a great job of using their entire team to serve their customers," my mentor continued. "Once you're seated, your server will usually come and introduce himself or herself before taking your drink order. If your server is tied up with another table when you're seated, the hostess or host will take your drink order.

"There's a high probability that your food will not be brought to your table by your server. Each member of their team has been taught that if they walk by the food counter and see an order ready to be delivered, they are to pick it up and take it to the customer."

"Now that you mention it, I remember this happening at a

restaurant that Lisa and I visited several weeks ago," I interrupted. "I also remember thinking that it was unusual that our server did not bring our food. I bet they had the same team process that your favorite restaurant used."

"Another sign of a restaurant using team service is how they clear your empty dishes and fill your drink glasses. Whenever a team member passed by our table, they were looking to see if you needed anything. If you had an empty glass, they would ask what you were drinking and get you a refill," Sam explained, "and I remember hearing Bill Marriott say that the bottom line to excellent customer service was to serve the hot food hot, the cold food cold, and to keep the glasses full.

"I'll also bet you've been at a restaurant that did not practice team service," Sam said. "For example, how many times have you needed a drink refill and asked a different server for a refill as they passed your table? What were you likely to hear?"

"I'll let your server know," I responded. "That's usually what they say...if they stop and respond to your request at all."

"That's right. It would've been just as easy for them to refill your drink themselves," Sam concluded.

"I can see that system working for a restaurant, but how does it apply in an office environment?" I asked.

"I'm glad you asked," Sam replied. "With most teams, there are days when individual team members are overwhelmed with work and other days when there is time to relax a bit. The key is to encourage your staff to aggressively look for ways they can help each other when they have downtime. Many people feel that they are on their own when providing services to a customer. The truth is that no one is an island and the more you involve your teammates, including leadership, in serving the customer, the better service you will be able to provide and the happier your customer will be.

Sam continued with another example. "During my early years, I managed a department where the sales team's compensation was based on their individual sales. About that same time, I was in the middle of buying furniture for a new home that Becky and I had built in Orlando. We had been in the furniture store several times and had been working with a particular sales associate. Becky had finalized her selections, and we were ready to purchase."

"I bet I know where this is going," I interjected. "Your salesperson was not in that day, and you had difficulty placing your order."

Sam laughed. "I guess you've had a similar experience! We spent the next hour trying to find a salesperson who was willing to help us. At that store, salespeople apparently were paid 100 percent on commission, and they had no process in place to share commissions if they assisted a customer that had been 'registered' to another sales associate."

He paused to take a sip of coffee and to watch as I furiously scribbled notes on what he had just said.

"We ended up going down the road to another furniture store to place our order that afternoon," Sam continued. "I felt bad for our original salesperson, but I had a problem giving my business to a company that encouraged behavior that did not benefit the customer."

"So what do you do when you run into someone in your organization who's unwilling to work with the rest of the team?" I wondered aloud. ·

"That can be tricky, especially if that person is talented and does a good job with their individual assignments," Sam said. "The first step in eliminating this self-centered behavior is to make it very clear to that employee that their success is going to be measured in part by how well they work with the rest of the team. Work with them to point out behavior that is inappropriate," Sam continued, "like ignoring customer requests — of any kind."

"What do you do if that doesn't work and the person is still a disruption to the rest of the team?" I asked, knowing that I had a member of my leadership team who definitely was not a team player.

"There comes a time when the best thing for the well-being of the entire team is to remove this employee," Sam responded. "I've had to do this on several occasions, and as painful as that whole scene may be to think about and carry out, the positive impact on the rest of the team was immediately noticed."

"Can I move that non-team player into a position where they don't have to deal with others?" I asked.

"Well," Sam began, "there aren't many positions in any company that don't require teamwork. In my experience, you're better off getting rid of this employee. The rest of the team will recognize that teamwork is a valued skill and will strive to help their teammates succeed. A self-centered member of a team can poison the attitude of the rest of the employees and diminish the quality of service given to the customer — and it can happen in a matter of days," he concluded.

"Okay, got it. And I have another question about teams. How do you get your frontline workers and leadership to work together as a team?"

"That leads me to another very important secret when it comes to delivering excellent service," Sam said. "I had a problem with my meal at a restaurant once. This particular establishment had a policy that any time a customer was not pleased or became upset, the server was instructed to bring it to the attention of the manager."

"I have a feeling that in our culture, frontline employees would be afraid they would be punished by their supervisor if they found out a customer was unhappy," I inserted.

"That's what keeps most organizations from ever using the tool of team service. You have to work with your leaders so they won't have a tendency to jump to conclusions. Instead, teach them to focus on taking care of the customer first. If the employee needs some coaching, that can be done after the customer is satisfied," Sam continued. "But back to my story.

"The server alerted his manager, and he immediately came to our table to find out what needed to happen to make things right. Translating this to a corporate scenario, there are similar times in any business where it is effective to bring the manager into the discussion with a customer. Why? Because, for some reason, a customer is more likely to respect the opinion of someone in a leadership position."

"It may be a subconscious reflex, but I always act differently when a supervisor walks up or gets on the phone," I agreed.

"Even if they were upset with the frontline worker, a customer may calm down once they get to talk with their supervisor. Taking a lesson from human nature, then, a great organization learns to place the needs of the customer above any individual concerns or needs," Sam said, making the solution to my seemingly complex problem astonishingly simple.

"I'll start working with my leadership team on this concept today," I responded.

"Well, Brett, I guess it's time to wrap up this session," Sam said, glancing at his watch.

"Sam, I can't thank you enough, not only for our meeting this morning, but also for encouraging me to keep our appointment. But before I go, let me summarize our main points for today:

1. The customer will benefit when an entire team is used to deliver the product or service.

2. All policies and procedures should be developed to encourage teamwork.

3. Employees who are not able to become team players should be removed.

4. When a team works together to service the customer, everyone wins.

5. Use leadership team members when needed to meet the needs of the customer."

"I think you got it!" Sam responded as we stood to go back into the house. "Next week we'll be talking about a critical aspect of satisfying your customer. It deals with setting correct expectations and then meeting or exceeding them."

"Don't worry. I'll be here bright and early next Monday. See you then," I said as I walked to my car.

The Seventh Monday

Be Realistic and Optimistic

I t was hard to believe that I had been meeting with Sam for six weeks.

I awoke ready and eager to make the short trip to the coast for my Monday morning session. As I drove to the beach house, I realized — for the first time — that I was no longer anxious about my new position. That anxiety had been replaced with a sense of excitement and anticipation. I was actually having fun implementing many of the new ideas that I had learned from Sam over the past six weeks.

In just a few short weeks on the job, I felt my team was also seeing the potential for our organization and the excellent guest service that we were capable of providing.

I arrived on time and met Sam at the door.

"How are you doing, Brett?" Sam asked as we shook hands and started for the kitchen to fill our mugs with hot coffee.

"What a week! I can't remember a week when I accomplished so much," I exclaimed.

Sam chuckled. "I've always found that when you take that time for preparation and planning, the rest of the week seems to go much smoother. I'm glad you experienced that yourself."

"When I left you last week, I was charged up and ready to start implementing some changes to develop a team approach to customer service. I met with my leadership team and brought them up to speed on what we had discussed.

"They all seemed open to the assignment of finding another member of the team outside their area of expertise and spending two hours with them to observe their job. We met again on Friday afternoon, and I could already see the change in their attitudes!

"We went around the table and shared our experiences. I started hearing things like, 'I never knew that the custodial staff did so much. I now realize that they have to know our products and attractions better than almost anyone. I used to think they just picked up trash and cleaned the grounds.'"

"That's a good sign," Sam replied. "Having a healthy appreciation for each other is a key ingredient to effective teams."

"They also started showing an interest in each other's challenges and even offered to help provide some temporary assistance to one area that was experiencing a staffing crisis," I continued.

I was proud of my team's accomplishments.

"One more thing…several weeks ago I formed a team of

frontline workers and a few leaders to evaluate our customer feedback process. I explained how it was important to have a closed loop and that the new process should include some accountability steps. They developed a process similar to what we had discussed during our Monday morning meeting — using guest feedback cards and some random interviews with guests to gather data. The group also made it easy for any employee to turn in suggestions that they may have heard from discussions with guests.

"My leadership team now receives a simple report each week with comments, both good and bad, and the entire team discusses the suggestions and determines if it is something we can fix."

I found myself breathless as I excitedly ticked off what was going right at the office.

"I can tell you're feeling better about being the director of Guest Services," Sam responded with a smile. "But have you run into any employees who are resistant to these new changes?"

"I've had a couple of people I'm keeping my eye on, but most of the employees are excited to have a fresh direction and something to work on," I replied.

Sam freshened his coffee and said, "Thanks for the report. It sounds like you're making giant strides on fine-tuning the organization, but now let's get busy with today's topic. Do you remember what we were going to discuss?"

"I believe it was dealing with setting expectations."

"Right. Let me start by giving you an illustration."

"Good. I always find it easier to apply what we talk about when I can remember your stories."

"I want to paint two pictures for you," Sam began. "In the first example, a friend of mine — Betsy Cline — needed some work done on her car. She decided to drop it off at the dealership that was near her job. As she pulled up in the service lane, she was greeted by a friendly service advisor with 'Scott' embroidered on his shirt. He asked her name and what he could do to help her that day.

"Betsy carefully described the noise her vehicle had begun making when she turned sharp corners. Scott must've heard that description many times before, because he immediately guessed that she would need some work on her front axle. Most likely the c.v. boot needed to be replaced. Sam related Betsy's story as I sipped my coffee.

"Scott knew that the service department had done this repair many times, and most of the time they could complete the job in a few hours. He took down some information from Betsy and said, 'Mrs. Cline, if it's convenient, you can pick up your car during your lunch hour.' Betsy responded, 'That would be great. It'll let me get to my workout on time this evening.'"

"The dealership gave Betsy a ride to work, and Scott got the car in a service bay to start the repair. His diagnosis was correct, so he ordered the part. They went on to work on other vehicles while they waited for the part to be delivered. The morning went by quickly, and at 11:00, he noticed that the part for Betsy's car had not yet arrived. He made a call to the parts store and found out that the order had been delivered to the wrong dealership.

Scott reluctantly picked up the phone and called Betsy to let her know that her car would not be ready until 5:00 p.m."

"I bet she wasn't very happy," I offered.

"You're exactly right," Sam continued. "In fact, she told the service rep she had already changed a luncheon appointment and made arrangements to have someone drop her off at the dealership, maybe to make him feel guilty that he hadn't delivered what he'd promised. Anyway, Scott apologized and went back to his work.

"Now let's paint the second picture," Sam said as he continued his illustration.

"Suppose Betsy had taken her car to be serviced and Scott had made the same diagnosis. Scott knows that in the large majority of cases, he gets the work done before noon, but he decides to be a bit cautious. 'Mrs. Cline, your car will be ready after work. Is 5:00 p.m. okay with you?'

"'Sure,' she said. 'That'll be fine.'

"At about 10:30 that morning Scott realized that the repair was going as planned and Mrs. Cline's car would be ready by noon. He picked up the phone and gave her a call. 'Mrs. Cline?' Scott asked as Betsy answered the phone. 'Yes. This is Betsy.'

"Scott continued, 'This is Scott from the dealership. I have some good news. Your car is going to be ready at noon if you want to drop by and pick it up at lunchtime.'" Sam continued, using his best impersonation of Scott and Betsy.

"Betsy was thrilled. 'That'll be great. I'll have my friend drop me off after lunch.'

"'See you then.' Scott responded."

Sam finished his story, then looked at me and asked, "Okay, Brett, which picture do you think made a satisfied customer?"

"Obviously the second. Your friend Betsy was pleasantly surprised when the car was done ahead of schedule," I replied.

"What was the difference?" Sam asked.

"I suppose it was the way in which the customer's expectations were set and met or not met," I answered.

"You're right. In the first example, Scott was a bit optimistic and promised something that he could not always deliver. In the second scenario, he still thought he would meet the noon deadline, but he only committed to the normal 5:00 p.m. completion," Sam explained.

"Are you suggesting that we add 'fluff' to our schedules so that we are always assured of meeting them?" I asked.

"Good question, Brett," Sam replied, "and, surprisingly, the answer is no. You should always, always be realistic with your schedules, but set your deadlines so that you have a chance to exceed your customer's expectations. You can still work hard to get the project done according to your schedule, but you don't have to let the customer know about the earlier target," he explained.

I could relate what Sam was saying to a similar experience. "I guess it would be the same thing at our theme park if we posted a wait time of 15 minutes from a particular point in line when we knew it was, realistically, 25 minutes. We would be better off being a bit cautious and posting a 30-minute wait time. That way, the guests would be pleased when they arrived at the front of the line five to ten minutes ahead of the expected time."

"That's correct," Sam responded. "The same applies for wait times — in restaurants or any business. Remember the number one point we discussed during our first meeting. It was when people had to wait in line. Whenever you're serving customers, you want to be as accurate as possible so you don't scare away customers with an overly cautious seating time, but you should err slightly on the side of caution by giving times a bit longer than you expect. That way, when they're seated earlier than expected, your customers begin their dining experience with a positive."

"May I get a refill on my coffee?" I asked as we took a short break.

"Sure. This is a new flavor that Becky picked up at the market just the other day. Good, isn't it?

"Here's another question for you, Brett. Have you ever looked at a brochure for a hotel or some other location that you were thinking of visiting and made a reservation based on what you read or saw in the brochure?" Sam asked.

"Yes. One year we were going to get a place on the beach on Sanibel Island. We searched for hotels online, and I found one that seemed like a great deal. The room description talked about the separate bedroom and the 'partial ocean view,'" I said as I remembered a vacation trip from several years back.

"What happened when you got there?" Sam asked.

"Well, the second room was only possible after we pulled an old, partially broken flexible partition from one wall to the other. It didn't latch, so the kids were constantly peeking around the corner. They thought it was great fun!" I continued.

"As for the 'partial ocean view,' I could only see a very tiny glimpse of the ocean if I stood on tiptoe and leaned my head over the balcony railing." I laughed as I thought about that day of many "discoveries."

"I bet you weren't laughing by day's end," Sam said with a smile.

"No, I wasn't. We ended up cutting our stay short and moved down the road to a different resort where we could actually see the ocean and the sunset."

"That's a great example for my next point. Sometimes our sales and marketing department may paint an inaccurate picture of our products or services. Granted, they're not trying to mislead intentionally, but they do tend to exaggerate the benefits and leave out important factors.

"As director of Guest Services, it's part of your job to make sure your organization is delivering on the advertised experience. You'll know from your guest feedback mechanisms if you're consistently missing the mark at meeting guest expectations," Sam explained.

"If your company offers a great experience for your guests, then your brochure should focus on giving all future guests an accurate picture of what they should expect," Sam continued.

"Then you can throw in some of those little extra things to exceed their expectations."

"Like that person at the pool I mentioned during our visit to a competing property," I recalled. "That resort didn't advertise that they would provide sunscreen if you forgot yours, but they used that extra bit of attention to surprise us and make our experience special."

"In summary, don't let your marketing department write a check that your frontline staff can't cash," Sam said with a chuckle. "It's an easy hole to fall into."

During the pause, I digested the great information Sam had once again provided.

"Now, why don't you go over what we discussed today?"

"Sure. Here are the highlights of today's discussion:

1. Be careful to set expectations accurately. If possible, leave room to surprise your customers by exceeding their expectations.

2. Don't pad numbers or time estimates excessively, but give yourself a 95 percent or better chance to meet or beat the estimate.

3. Give potential customers an accurate picture of your product or service. Don't get carried away with marketing materials only to have a guest leave disappointed."

"That's all good business — and one more thing. Let your directors and managers set accurate expectations for you. Many leaders think it is their job to constantly push and to never be content with the estimate your team gives you. It's a leader's job to get the team to constantly improve and enhance performance, but many times your subordinates will feel pressure to agree to a deadline they don't believe they'll make. This only leads to all of you being frustrated when the deadline has to be adjusted," Sam explained.

"That's something I'll have to watch out for," I replied. "Coming from the financial office, where we're always trying to do more with less, I can see myself pushing my team beyond what is realistic. Thanks for that tip.

"Sam, I can't believe our last session is next week!" I said. "I don't know what I'll do without my coffee and time at the beach each week with you."

"Don't worry, Brett. I'm not going to abandon you. I've enjoyed this time probably more than you, and it's been fun to remember all those examples from my career," Sam replied.

"So do you have a topic for us to discuss next week?" I asked, expecting a topic worthy of a grand finale.

Sam responded, "Guest Recovery!"

"Oh," I replied. "Reality just set in. I guess new policies don't always fix problems, and sometimes things don't go as planned. I've been so excited about my team's progress that I didn't think about the times we'll make a mistake."

"This is one of the most important processes to ensure long-term success and repeat business. And just a hint…I enjoy this topic more than any of the previous ones, so be ready for some stories and some good examples. That's why I saved it for last," Sam said with a smile as I left the front porch.

"See you next week!" I said.

"I'll be here. Now I have to head to the course to 'recover' from that bad round I played last week," Sam chuckled.

The Eighth Monday

Recover Right

I had mixed emotions as I made the drive to the beach for the eighth week in a row. Part of me was going to miss the weekly sessions with Sam and the wisdom he imparted each time we met. Another part of me was ready to totally concentrate on putting into practice all I had learned the past eight weeks.

To be honest, I felt myself reaching the point of information overload and realized why Sam had suggested meeting for only eight sessions. Any more and I may have become frustrated as I continued to process new ideas each week without an extended amount of time to implement them.

I think my car could have made the two left turns and then a right turn into Sam's neighborhood without my hands on the wheel. As usual, Sam was waiting for me on the front porch as I pulled around the corner.

"Hello, Brett!" Sam greeted me as I opened my car door.

"Hi, Sam. As usual, it's good to see

you." I shook Sam's hand as I stepped onto the porch. "What is that I smell?" I asked.

"Becky thought we should have more than just coffee on our final week," Sam explained. "She made a full breakfast for us. I hope you're hungry!"

Becky was a great cook! Lisa and I had been to their house years earlier for a fine meal. Today, Becky had a table set out on the deck. It was a beautiful morning. The breeze was blowing, and we could feel the surf in the air.

"Thanks for breakfast, Becky!" I said as she brought out platters of crepes, bacon and homemade cinnamon rolls.

"It's my pleasure," Becky replied.

"Won't you join us for breakfast?"

"Thanks, but I've already sampled everything as it came out of the oven. Enjoy your breakfast," Becky said as she returned to the house.

This morning I was particularly eager to tell Sam about my week. "Before we get started on guest recovery, I want to tell you about something my team accomplished."

"Sure. Go ahead. I have all the time you need today. My foursome canceled," Sam said.

"Several weeks ago we talked about onstage versus backstage. I took that information back to my leadership team and asked them for their ideas on how we could do a better job in this area," I explained.

"What did they come up with?" Sam was immediately interested.

"We discussed several ideas, but ended up creating an onstage review team. This team of six individuals is charged with walking the property at least once each week to help spot backstage activities that are in view of our guests," I continued. "If they identify something that needs our attention, they're empowered to bring it to the manager on duty over that area."

"How did you decide who to put on this team?" Sam asked.

"I asked each of my six directors to nominate one person. We reviewed the names and made a few adjustments to ensure we had a balance of departments and levels within the organization.

"The team includes several members who are in support roles that normally do not interact with our guests. And you'll be pleased with this next item. In order to keep a fresh look at our operation, the team members are only allowed to serve for three months before they rotate off and are replaced with six new sets of eyes," I said proudly.

"The team meets once a month to discuss what they've found and what corrective action they observed. They also prepare a report for the executive team to review. You should see how excited the team members are to be involved with the review team! It has quickly changed the attitudes of many of our frontline employees and has made them more attentive to the needs of our guests," I concluded.

"That sounds like a great idea, Brett. You'll have to let me know how they're doing in six months. The toughest thing I found in my own experience is to sustain that attitude and attention to detail," Sam offered, "but something I found helpful to use was an old truism that says, 'Customers don't forget attitudes.' This includes the attitudes of everyone in your company — not just your frontliners, but everyone from the receptionist, the secretary and even drivers or messengers your company uses.

"Now, before we go further, do you want anything else to eat?"

"No thanks. I'm already getting full from this great breakfast!" I responded. "You better have some good stories today, or I may fall asleep!"

"I'll do my best," Sam laughed. "I'm sure you'll agree that even the best organizations make mistakes once in a while. We're all human, and even the best plans and processes go wrong when you combine your employees and your customers," Sam began.

"Sure. I've made my share of mistakes in my career," I agreed.

"How an organization responds to, or 'recovers,' from a guest complaint or a service blunder is the single biggest factor that separates the average company from the exceptional.

"That being said, have you ever received a call from someone wanting you to participate in a short survey?" Sam asked.

"Sure. Who hasn't? And they always seem to call during dinner!"

"Those companies are spending a lot of money trying to find out how you feel about their products. The strange thing is that some of those same companies have no process in place to deal with feedback given by their current customers. When you have a customer complain about your product or service, a light should go off in your head for two reasons:

1. They may be pointing out an area you need to fix to become a more effective and profitable company.

2. You now have the opportunity to interact with this person and turn them into a loyal customer."

"I'm sure you have some great illustrations for this topic!" I stated.

"I sure do. Let me start with one where the company missed their opportunity," Sam replied. "About 20 years ago, Becky and I were on a business trip in San Antonio, Texas. We were out for a fun evening and had chosen to have dinner at a restaurant that specialized in ribs. It was located on the famous San Antonio Riverwalk, and we had a table a few feet from the water's edge."

"I bet that was nice. Lisa and I have been thinking about taking a trip there someday," I said.

"We were almost finished with the main part of our meal when another waiter was walking by. He tripped and dumped a plateful of ribs on Becky's dress!" Sam continued animatedly.

"I bet that waiter was embarrassed."

"I'm sure he was...so embarrassed that he disappeared, and we never saw him again," Sam replied.

"Eventually, the manager heard what had happened and came to our table and apologized. Do you know what his 'recovery' solution was?" Sam asked.

"By your tone, I bet it wasn't sufficient," I responded.

"His only response was to tell us, 'If you send me your dry cleaning bill, I will reimburse you for the expense.'"

"You're kidding," I was incredulous.

"It gets worse. They then proceeded to deliver the check for the full amount of our meal," Sam said, able to laugh about it now. "It was fully 15 years before I set foot in that restaurant chain again, even though I often had a hunger for ribs — and theirs were some of the best we'd ever eaten," Sam concluded.

"Now, I don't want to dwell on the negative, so let me give you a positive example of guest recovery." Once again, Sam was on a roll. This was obviously a favorite subject.

"When Becky and I first moved to Orlando, we went with some friends to a restaurant that served Caribbean-style food. We were there for lunch, and I had ordered a sandwich, barbecue meat on a large roll. About two bites into the sandwich, I discovered that I had received some 'bonus' material. There was something in the meat that did not belong there. I'll spare you the details," Sam laughed as I squirmed.

"I got my server's attention and showed him the problem. The next thing I knew, the manager on duty was at our table, apologizing for the problem. Remember a couple of weeks ago when I told you about using management to deliver team service?"

"Was this the example you were talking about?" I replied.

"Sure was. The server had immediately informed the manager, who then came to our table to 'recover' on behalf of their restaurant. I was expecting a free meal or maybe a complimentary dessert, but when I got the bill, he had taken all the charges for our entire table off, making the meal on the house."

"Wasn't that costly for them to do that?" I asked, the former financial executive side of me coming out.

Sam continued. "I figured they probably gave away $50 worth of food at their cost during that incident. That was six years ago, and I've been back to their restaurant no less than 25 times. Becky and I take almost all of our company to this place, and I've had several large business dinner meetings there. I've used this example more than 50 times in front of thousands of people when I talked to groups about customer service, so I guarantee that many others went to this restaurant based on my referral. If I use conservative estimates, the restaurant has gained more than $10,000 in business because they did an exceptional job of 'recovering' from that first mistake."

"Awesome! I'd take that return on investment any day!" I laughed.

Sam then added, "They saw the opportunity to turn what could've been a very bad experience into one that converted me into one of their most loyal customers. I may or may not have been so impressed if the problem had not happened in the first place."

"So are you suggesting that we intentionally mess up to provide these opportunities for recovery?" I joked.

"No, no, no. But, unfortunately, most organizations provide these opportunities naturally without setting them up," Sam chuckled. "But when they do happen, your entire team should be ready to spring into action to make things right for the customer."

"Okay, I've done most of the talking so far, so now it's your turn, and I have a question for you," Sam continued. "What do you think is the most underutilized tool for recovering from a mistake with your customers?"

"I know this one," I replied. "I bet it's saying you're sorry to the customer and admitting fault when that's appropriate."

"You got it. For some reason, those two words — I'm sorry — get stuck in people's throats," Sam pointed out. "Both in our personal lives and in business, we find it hard to simply say, 'I'm sorry.'"

"And the best thing is, this solution doesn't cost anything," I added.

Sam took it from there. "Many times when a customer is upset about something that has happened with your organization, the first thing they want to hear is, 'I'm sorry.' It's amazing how those two simple words can disarm an angry guest or customer. I know in my own experience, I've called a customer service line to complain about a product or service. The longer the conversation proceeds before the employee admits some fault, the more upset I become. If they had just started with a simple 'Mr. Baldwin, I'm sorry that this happened to you. How can we make it right?', I would've backed off and been very reasonable with them," he explained.

"I can relate," I added. "Some people spend more time coming up with excuses or passing the buck than just admitting fault and moving forward."

"One more thing I'd like for you to remember, Brett. If you take care of your customers, they'll take care of your business."

"Definitely food for thought — and for sharing with my team," I decided.

As was his habit, Sam glanced at his watch. "I see it's time to wrap up for today, so why don't you take a shot at summarizing this last topic?" Sam remarked.

"Okay. I can see why you left this topic for the end. Without guest recovery, you're never going to reach that top level of service. With that in mind, these are the main points I'm going to take home from today's session:

1. We need to look at guest complaints as valuable feedback that gives us an opportunity to improve our services.

2. The recovery needs to be immediate and appropriate for the mistake.

3. A successful 'recovery' can turn an upset person into a loyal customer, more than paying back the cost to fix the original mistake.

4. We must develop a culture where frontline staff members are comfortable involving their leaders when it is in the best interest of the customer.

5. Learn to say 'I'm sorry' when appropriate. This can relax a customer and let you solve the problem before things get too intense."

"I can tell you got this topic!" Sam said, showing pleasure in successfully guiding his student.

I couldn't believe that I'd finished my last session with Sam. It goes without saying that I was already finding my new position challenging and rewarding.

"Sam, I can't thank you enough for taking the past eight Monday mornings to meet with me. I have a spiral notebook filled with notes from our sessions — and I'm actually looking forward to implementing many of the ideas and suggestions we've discussed with my new staff," I said.

"I'm glad you feel better about your new position," Sam said. He was obviously gratified with my enthusiasm. "I've enjoyed your company, and our discussions have made me think of a few new examples and tools to share as I continue to provide customer service training for my clients."

"May I come back and see you for a refresher course once in a while?" I asked.

"Why don't we set up another visit in a couple of months?" Sam suggested. "If you like, I could come out to your office and meet some of your team members."

"That would be great!" I replied, excited about Sam experiencing some of our excellent service. "Why don't you and Becky come out to the park? Hopefully you'll see some of the things we've talked about actually put into practice."

"Brett, I have one more assignment," Sam said with a smile. "As you develop your experience in customer service and have success at leading your new organization, I want you to be open to mentoring someone else if the opportunity presents itself."

"I'm not qualified now, but I hope to be by this time next year," I stammered, somewhat surprised by Sam's assignment. "But you have my word. I'll do whatever I can to help someone else along."

Sam's wife joined us in the kitchen as we were bringing in our dishes. "I'm going to miss seeing you every Monday, Brett."

"Believe me, I'm going to miss my visits, our discussions and the coffee! And thanks for the breakfast this morning. I think I need to walk home to work off the calories," I laughed.

I headed to my car and turned to say goodbye. "Goodbye, Sam. I'll give you a call in a few months to schedule our follow-up visit. Your influence will extend to many people and thousands of our guests. Thank you."

Final Thoughts

The following Monday, I was so accustomed to getting up early and meeting with Sam that I decided to spend that time in my office reviewing my notes and jotting down a short summary of the lessons I had learned from my mentor. In doing so, I created a simple checklist that I hope you will find helpful. Believe it or not, I still refer to it regularly to make sure I stay on track.

Listen Up

✔ Customer service is critical to a successful operation. Most unhappy customers will not tell you they are not pleased, but will simply take their business elsewhere.

✔ It is a good investment to spend resources in an effort to retain your existing customers. Your best customer is your current customer.

✔ It is important to have a complete closed-loop process to gather feedback, take action and then respond to the customer.

✔ Use a combination of internal-feedback tools and external resources to obtain a good balance of data. An independent assessment is a good way to obtain an accurate picture of how you are doing.

✔ All leaders should schedule regular time with frontline workers and customers to stay in touch with the issues and challenges.

Scout the Competition

✔ The number one customer turnoff is a long line. Minimize the time your customers are waiting for an attraction or some other service.

✔ Scouting the competition results in one of two responses:

♦ You will have pride in your work because you were better than the competition.

♦ You will strive to improve in an area to reach and surpass your competition.

✔ "Lagniappe" – always give the customer a little extra.

✔ The trailing edge prospers. You don't always have to be the first to do something. Capitalize on the other guy's hard work and improve on it.

✔ Trade shows can be an efficient way to scout your competition and come up with new ideas.

Chisel a Culture of Accountability

✔ Make sure all employees are trained and can answer a question in their area of expertise. If customers do not feel that an employee knows what they are talking about, they will find someone else who does.

✔ Cross-train all staff members. Each employee at our company should know the basics about our products and services and whom to call to get more information for a customer. This also creates a backup person for each critical process.

✔ Create Quick Reference Fact Sheets to help everyone understand what each department does and whom to call for more information.

✔ Rotate your leaders to different areas. This will help them keep fresh, gain new ideas, and uncover problems that may not be found otherwise.

Know Your Stuff!

✔ The first step in developing accountability is to fulfill your responsibilities as an employer to properly train each employee.

✔ There are three important aspects of an initial training program:

    a. **Culture.** All employees, (and critical contractors) should know the history and values that shape your company. This includes setting expectations on how your customers are to be treated.

b. Job Training. Employees should know the details of their assigned jobs and should be able to carry out their duties effectively.

c. Cross-training. Each employee at any level in the organization, including your receptionist or valet attendant, should know the key services and products that your company offers to clients.

✔ Create a process to analyze customer feedback to spot trends and take action.

✔ Don't be afraid to discipline and terminate someone who is not performing. The good employees will appreciate it when you hold people accountable.

✔ Conduct regular balanced reviews and keep the process simple. Consider using a simple three-part review form:

1. Positive Feedback. What did the employee do that was excellent or above your expectations?

2. Constructive Feedback. What should the employee improve, start doing or stop doing?

3. Job-Specific Goals. Develop in advance four to five goals with specific measurements, and record whether the employee met the goal, did not meet the goal, or partially met the goal.

Keep Backstage Things Backstage

✔ "Onstage" refers to things that the customer is supposed to hear or see.

✔ "Backstage" refers to things that are done behind the scenes where the customer does not hear or see them.

✔ Train employees to always respect the customer.

✔ It is the leader's ultimate job to maintain a high standard of service and ensure that backstage activities are truly behind the scenes.

✔ Use a Mystery Guest service to provide a fresh look at the company's environment and service quality.

✔ Consider creating an onstage committee to review operations to spot things that are not supposed to be visible to the customer.

Get Off Your Island!

✔ The customer will benefit when an entire team is utilized to deliver the product or service.

✔ Policies and procedures should be developed to encourage teamwork, especially when it comes to how you compensate your employees.

✔ Employees who are not able to become team players should be removed.

✔ When a team works together to service the customer, everyone wins.

✔ Learn to use leadership team members when needed to meet the needs of the customer.

Be Realistic and Optimistic

✔ Be careful to set expectations accurately. If possible, leave some room to surprise your customer by exceeding expectations.

✔ Don't pad your numbers or time estimates excessively, but give yourself a 95 percent or better chance to meet or beat the estimate.

✔ Give your potential customers an accurate picture of your product or service. Don't get carried away with marketing materials only to have a guest leave disappointed.

Recover Right

✔ Look at guest complaints as valuable feedback that gives you an opportunity to improve your services.

✔ The recovery needs to be appropriate to fit the mistake.

✔ A successful recovery can turn an upset person into a loyal customer, which will more than pay back the cost of fixing the original mistake.

✔ Develop a culture where the frontline staff is comfortable involving its leaders to deal with problems when it is in the best interest of the customer.

✔ Learn to say "I'm sorry" when appropriate. This can relax a customer and let you solve the problem before things get too intense.

This looks like the end of my story of how Sam helped me prepare for my challenging new position, but in a way, it is only the beginning.

I still have a lot to learn, but those eight Monday mornings with Sam gave me a running start on my new job and helped me make some positive changes as director of Guest Services.

And someday, if you find yourself in a similar position, I hope you can have a friend and mentor like Sam to turn to for advice and coaching. It's made a difference for me. It can do the same for you.

Customer Centered
Consulting Group, Inc.

Customer Centered Consulting Group, Inc. was formed in 1999 to help companies of all sizes improve their effectiveness through enhanced customer service, strong leadership, and simple processes. With offices in Florida and Texas, the company's services are focused in the customer service area.

♦ **Customer service assessments** – Perform an objective review of your customer service as seen from the eye of a customer, client, or partner. To perform this assessment, we utilize surveys, "mystery guest" observations, focus groups, and a review of internal policies and procedures.

♦ **Customer service training** – Provide half-day and full day interactive training sessions to re-focus the attention on the customer and reinforce your policies and procedures that deal with the treatment of your customers.

♦ **Customer feedback process creation** – Create guest and customer surveys along with the internal process to put this information to work in your organization.

♦ **Keynote addresses** – Address your convention, conference, or internal meetings on topics of customer service and leadership.

In addition to the customer service area, Customer Centered Consulting Group, Inc. provides services in the human resources and business operations arenas.

If you are interested in learning more about these services, please visit the web site, call, or send an email to **info@cccginc.com**.

Customer Centered Consulting Group, Inc.
5729 Lebanon Dr., Suite 144-222
Frisco, TX 75034
(469) 633-9833 voice
(469) 633-9843 fax
www.cccginc.com

About the Authors

David Reed

Prior to founding Customer Centered Consulting Group, Inc., David served with Andersen Consulting, Exxon, and Walt Disney World. Using his unique ability to combine technical information with outstanding interpersonal skills, David Reed has made his mark on the business community by teaching companies of all sizes how to enhance organizational effectiveness and increase customer service.

David resides in Frisco, Texas and travels throughout the country helping schools, churches, corporations, and government agencies identify their strengths and weaknesses. Then, by working with leadership teams and teaching simple processes, he helps organizations create and implement common-sense solutions to their problems.

Well-known as a speaker and trainer in corporate America, David also has been a featured guest and expert on programs and panels exploring various customer service issues.

David Cottrell

President and CEO of CornerStone Leadership Institute, David is an internationally known leadership consultant, educator and speaker. His business experience includes senior management positions with Xerox and FedEx. He also led the successful turnaround of a chapter eleven company before founding CornerStone. David's 25-plus years of professional experience are reflected in fifteen highly acclaimed books and his reputation as a premier public speaker.

Other CornerStone Leadership Books:

Monday Morning Leadership is David Cottrell's best-selling book. It offers unique encouragement and direction that will help you become a better manager, employee, and person. **$12.95**

Goal Setting for Results addresses the fundamentals of setting and achieving your goal of moving yourself and your organization from where you are, to where you want (and need) to be! **$9.95**

136 Effective Presentation Tips is a powerful handbook providing 136 practical, easy to use tips to make every presentation a success. **$9.95**

Sticking To It: The Art of Adherence reveals the secret to success for high achieving organizations and provides practical advice on how you can win the game of business. **$9.95**

Listen Up, Sales & Customer Service is written from the perspective of a customer who cares enough to tell you the truth. This book maps a step-by-step pathway to long-lasting customer relationships. **$9.95**

Building Customer Loyalty provides 21 essential elements that build Customer Loyalty. You will also learn dozens of ways to strengthen your customer relationships. **$9.95**

Customer at the Crossroads offers a humorous and entertaining way to reinforce key customer service values. **$9.95**

180 Ways to Walk the Customer Service Talk is one resource that you will want to read and distribute to every person in your organization. It is packed with powerful strategies and tips to cultivate world-class customer service. **$9.95**

175 Ways to Get More Done in Less Time has 175 really good suggestions that will help you get things done faster...usually better. **$9.95**

Visit www.**cornerstoneleadership**.com
for additional books and resources.